IMAGES OF SPORT

SWANSEA RFC
SINCE 1945

IMAGES OF SPORT

SWANSEA RFC
SINCE 1945

BLEDDYN HOPKINS

TEMPUS

Frontispiece: Captain Stuart Davies (centre) is seen here celebrating the club's success in winning the Heinekin League in 1993/94. Stuart's teammates are seen in similarly joyous mood.

First published 2004

Tempus Publishing Limited
The Mill, Brimscombe Port,
Stroud, Gloucestershire, GL5 2QG
www.tempus-publishing.com

British Library Cataloguing in Publication Data.
A catalogue record for this book is available from the British Library.

ISBN 0 7524 3107 2

Typesetting and origination by Tempus Publishing Limited.
Printed in Great Britain.

Contents

Acknowledgements

The production of this book would not have been possible without the assistance of many people. First and foremost, special thanks go to David Price and Michelle Payne for their assistance with the many items of memorabilia loaned by the club. Also to John Harris who provided many of the photographs of the last twenty-five years and to Timothy Auty who made his vast private collection of photographs available to me.

Thanks also to David Farmer (author of *The Life and Times of Swansea RFC*), former players Dil Johnson, W.O. 'Billy' Williams and Eddie Burns, Stuart Rees of www.thewhitesrugby.com, Dai Richards of www.rugbyrelics.com, Phil Sumbler of www.jackarmy.net, Ian Milne (Swansea Schools Rugby Union), and the Swansea Reference Library.

Apologies if I have inadvertently omitted anyone from the above list.

Finally, thanks to Scott Gibbs for writing the foreword to the book. He has achieved much success in rugby union, including 53 Wales caps, triple British Lion honours (1993, 1997 and 2001), captained Swansea for a record equaling five consecutive seasons and captained the Neath/Swansea Ospreys regional team in 2003/04. In 1997, his man-of-the-series performance in South Africa with the British Lions culminated in his winning the Welsh Sports Personality of the Year award. Scott also had a brief but distinguished rugby league career.

Bleddyn Hopkins

This is the 1973/74 squad in their special centenary kit. From left to right, back row: Roger Blyth, Neil Webb, Phil Llewellyn, Mike James, Mervyn Davies, Geoff Wheel, Roger Hyndman. Middle row: David Price, Gordon Morris, Dudley Thomas, Peter Thomas, Mark Keyworth, Rowe Harding, Trevor Evans, Darrel Cole, Alan Mages, Barry Clegg, Jim Trott, Gwyn White, Norman Blyth. Seated: Dickie Dobbs, Mike Yandle, Vivian Davies, Robert Dyer, Ieuan Evans, Bruce Barter, Gerwyn Jones, Eddie Rickard. Front row: Gwynfor Higgins, John Evans.

Foreword

Having enjoyed a successful period with the Swansea club, it is with considerable pleasure I write a foreword to this pictorial presentation, reflecting both the fortunes of the club and of some of its greatest players and occasions.

The first book in the series covered the many successes of the club from its formation through to 1945. This book traces the club's developments since 1945 right up to the present day.

Since its inception, Swansea has always been a leading club, both within Wales and on the international scene. The club became the first team to beat the Southern Hemisphere 'Big Three' (Australia, South Africa and New Zealand) and are renowned for having been pioneers in visiting countries all over the world.

The immediate post-war years brought only limited success, although a notable 6-6 draw was achieved against New Zealand in 1953 followed by a 9-8 victory against Australia in 1966. It was not until the club's centenary season in 1973/74, however, that the club became Merit Table Champions. Prior to my joining the club in 1991, Swansea had achieved further success as club champions in 1979/80, 1980/81, 1982/83 as well as being Welsh Cup winners in 1978.

The last decade or so has seen unprecedented success, including being league champions on four occasions (1991/92, 1993/94, 1997/98 and 2000/01) and Welsh Cup winners in 1995 and 1999.

I feel extremely proud to have been part of the club's most recent successes, including that memorable occasion on 4 November 1992 when the 'All Whites' defeated the World Champions Australia by 21 points to 6. I have also enjoyed being club captain for five consecutive seasons – a record shared with two of the greatest names in the club's history, namely Billy Bancroft and Billy Trew.

It has been a pleasure to play alongside some great 'All Whites' during the last decade, most notably Garin Jenkins, the Moriarty brothers, Stuart Davies, Colin Charvis, Robert Jones, Anthony Clement and Mark Taylor.

The author and compiler, Bleddyn Hopkins – who is incidentally a Merthyr man, but a devoted 'Jack' – is to be congratulated on his diligent researches in producing the book for publication. I can commend his work both to the rugby historian and enthusiast. It will rekindle memories of some of the club's special occasions and achievements and the deeds of its multitude of players, both famous and not so famous. Comparable books have already been published on other clubs, and we are indebted to Mr Hopkins for bringing the 'All Whites' into prominence.

Scott Gibbs

Introduction

Swansea 'All Whites' was originally an association football club formed in 1872. In 1874 it changed to rugby football and a year later joined with the existing cricket club to become Swansea Cricket & Football Club. The current title Swansea RFC Ltd dates from the age of professionalism (1995).

The club in 1881 became one of the eleven founder clubs of the Welsh Rugby Union and its home, the world-famous St Helen's ground, was formerly an international rugby venue (1882-1954) and equally famous as a cricket centre for Glamorgan County Cricket Club.

A total of 23 Swansea players have represented the British Lions and 158 have been capped since 1882 for Wales. Amongst this number are four of the most capped players of all time – Colin Charvis, Garin Jenkins, Robert Jones and Scott Gibbs, all with over 50 caps.

Since inception, Swansea has always been a leading club, both within Wales and on the international scene. The club won the Welsh cup on four occasions in the 1870s and 1880s. Early halcyon days were in the 'golden era' period of 1898 to 1914, when they were invincible in one season (1904/05) and Welsh champions on six other occasions. In this period both Australia (1908) and South Africa (1912) were defeated.

The inter-war years brought only limited success in the form of Welsh championship runners up achievements in 1928/29, 1929/30 and 1931/32 and the famous 11-3 victory against New Zealand in 1935. Swansea thus became the first club side to defeat the Southern Hemisphere 'Big Three' of Australia, South Africa and New Zealand.

The immediate post-Second World War years brought little success, other than a notable 6-6 draw with New Zealand in 1953 and later victory against Australia in 1966. It was not until the club's centenary season in 1973/74 that honours were achieved, in the form of them being crowned Merit Table champions. The team went on to win the Schweppes Cup in 1978 and this represented the start of a very successful five-year period, including being Anglo-Welsh champions in 1979/80 and 1982/83 and Merit Table champions in 1980/81.

Since the introduction of leagues in 1990/91, the club has headed the Welsh Premier Division on three occasions, the Welsh-Scottish League once, won the Challenge Cup twice (in 1995 and 1999) and been losing finalists on three other occasions. In 1992 the club recorded a memorable victory over the reigning World Champions, Australia, by 21 points to 6. In 1995/96, Swansea reached the semi-final stage of the European Cup.

The club has been a pioneer in touring foreign countries. This began with France in 1899. In the years after the Second World War this has extended to Italy, Germany, Rumania (they were the first club side to tour behind the 'Iron Curtain'), Czechoslovakia and Switzerland. In recent seasons there have been tours to the Far East (1979), California (1981), West Indies (1984), Kenya and Zimbabwe (1987), Florida (1990) and Canada (1992) – together with short tours to France, Germany, Italy, Switzerland, Czechoslovakia, Ireland and Holland. On their pre-season tour to Switzerland in 1976/77, Swansea changed for two of their games in dressing rooms in Switzerland and took a short walk through two sets of customs control points to play on pitches in France!

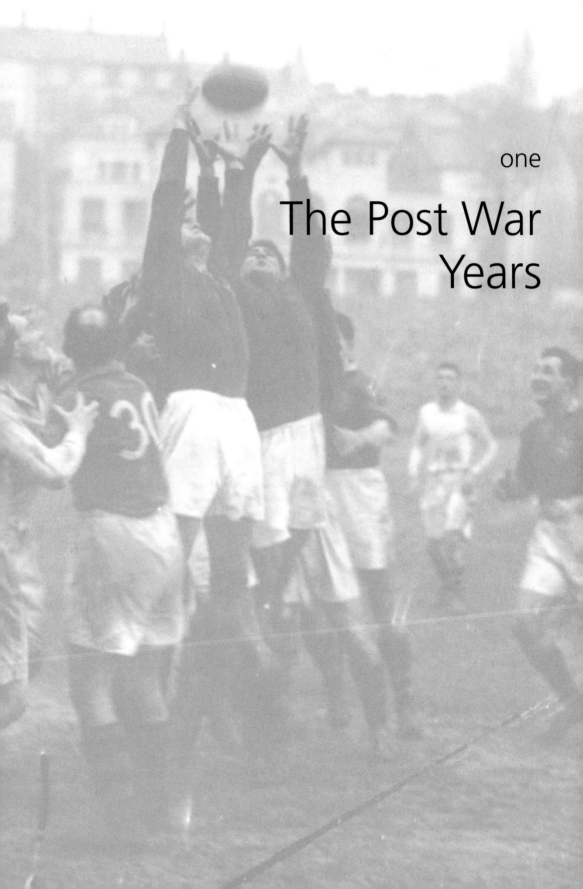

one

The Post War
Years

Having surrendered the lease to St Helen's at the commencement of hostilities, Swansea Council was required to approve the continuation of rugby from 1945/46. Fortunately, it duly did so and the first game at the ground after the war took place on 22 September 1945 versus archrivals Llanelli, which Swansea won by 19 points to 6.

In the Exiles XV game (26 January 1946), T. Egan changed sides with Guy Addenbroke at half time and scored a try for Swansea in the second half. Ernest Bevin, the Foreign Secretary, kicked off the game at Aberavon on 16 March 1946.

At the conclusion of the first post-war season the club's playing record read as follows: played 33, won 18, drawn 4, lost 11, points for 358, points against 244. Wing Guy Addenbroke achieved the season's most appearances, tries and points with 30, 20 and 65 respectively.

ST. HELEN'S GROUND, SWANSEA, SATURDAY, OCT. 27th, 1945, kick-off 3-0

SWANSEA

RUGBY MATCH
(Entire Proceeds for SERVICE'S CHARITIES)
SOUVENIR PROGRAMME 3d.

NEW ZEALAND EXPEDITIONARY FORCE

On 27 October 1945, Swansea played the New Zealand Expeditionary Force and were well beaten 22-6. Swansea's points came from a Dil Johnson try and a Gilbert Parkhouse penalty.

The Swansea team that played the touring Barbarians on Easter Monday 1946. Six members of the touring New Zealand Expeditionary Force squad played in the game – three for each team – including Major Charles Saxton, Swansea's captain on the day who was to later return as manager of the touring New Zealand party in 1967. The final score was Swansea 6 Barbarians 11, with Swansea's points coming from tries by Guy Addenbroke and New Zealander R. Dobson.

From left to right, back row: Trevor Davies (committee), Tom Briggs, John Hopkins, Trevor Petherbridge, Wilf Harris (committee), Rees Williams, Jim Hunt, Tom Rees, Trevor Lewis, Dai Jones, J. Elwyn Watkins (committee). Middle row: Cliff Prosser (secretary), Gwyn Griffiths, Denzil Llewellyn, Major Charles Saxton (captain, NZ), Harry Payne, Len Davies, R.E. Dobson (NZ), Trevor Jones (referee). Front row: H.E. Cook (NZ), Guy Addenbroke.

This is the Swansea squad that toured Cornwall in September 1946. The club defeated Penzance 14-0 (14 September), Redruth 7-0 (16 September) and Falmouth 25-5 (17 September). The Cornish papers referred to Swansea as having provided a 'delightful exhibition of all-round rugby'. The tour was a particularly successful one for Guy Addenbroke, who scored a try hat-trick against Penzance in front of a 5,000 crowd and scored two more tries against Falmouth.

The 1946/47 squad with a playing record of: played 35, won 19, drawn 3, lost 13, points for 330, points against 236. During the season, trainer Bob Dowdle completed fifty years' service with the club. From left to right, inset: Billy Beynon, Bryn Evans, Tom Sullivan. Back row: Bob Dowdle (trainer), Denny Hunt (committee), Trevor Davies (committee), Tom Rees, Howard Jones, Dai Jones, Dil Johnson, John Rowland, Cliff Prosser (secretary), Roy Jones (committee). Seated: Graham Morse, Guy Addenbroke, Dai Glyn Davies, Dai John Davies (captain), Rees Williams, Tom Briggs, George Bateman (assistant trainer). Ground: Len Davies, Alun Thomas, George Beynon, E Griffiths.

Australia defeated Swansea by 11 points to 8 on 13 December 1947 in front of 30,000 spectators. A feature of the game was a long–distance try by Dil Johnson, who intercepted near the Swansea line and outstripped the opposition. The captain D. Glyn Davies succeeded with the conversion to add to a first-half Len Davies penalty. With barely five minutes of play left, Swansea were leading 8–3 and it looked as if the All Whites had once again achieved an outstanding victory, as in 1908, but it was not to be.

This is the Swansea team that faced Australia. From left to right, back row: Denny Hunt (committee), Dai Jones, Tom Gange, Doug Jones, Tom Briggs, David Swain, Alun Thomas, Arthur Perkins (assistant trainer). Middle row: Cliff Prosser (secretary), Len Shaw, Len Davies, Bryn Evans, Dai Glyn Davies (captain), Dil Johnson, John Rowland, John W. Jenkins. Front row: Denzil Jones, Frank Williams.

Australia secure line-out possession near their own five-yard line against Swansea.

Swansea and Australian players scramble for the ball near the dead-ball line.

This photograph is from the Cardiff versus Swansea game on 15 October 1949. As the club was formed on 17 October 1874, this was the nearest to the club's seventy-fifth anniversary. The two Swansea players giving chase to the ball are Hywel Hopkins (left) and Len Davies. Cardiff had eight internationals in their team and led 9-0 at half time, only for Swansea to eventually win 18-12.

The Swansea captain Bryn Evans is carried off by teammates in celebration of the magnificent victory at Cardiff, with the escorting policeman watching anxiously. Swansea had become the first Welsh club to defeat Cardiff at the Arms Park since 1947. The crowd of 40,000 was a record for a club game up to that time.

This is the Swansea squad that featured in the 1949/50 South & West Wales Young Wales annual seven-a-side tournament. From left to right: Ken Jones, Curtis Grove, Hubert Thomas, Alun Thomas, Clem Thomas, Len Blyth and Dil Johnson.

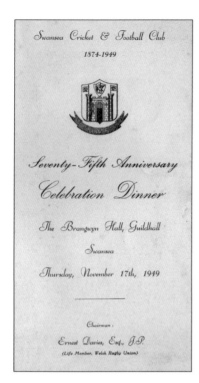

Programme and ticket for the club's seventy-fifth anniversary celebrations, held on 17 November 1949 at the Brangwyn Hall. Among former players in attendance were Billy Bancroft, 'Genny' Gordon and Will Joseph. Eric Evans, secretary of the Welsh Union declared, 'Swansea's contribution to rugby has been immeasurable'. At this time, Cliff Prosser BEM, was the sixth honorary secretary of the club since its inception and held the post from 1945 until 1955, when ill health forced his retirement. He had been instrumental in getting the club back on its feet after the atrocities of the Second World War and later became life vice president of the club. He was WRU President for 1966/67 and had been the 'District E' representative for a number of years prior to this.

The 1949/50 squad with a playing record of: played 43, won 29, drawn 3, lost 11, points for 481, points against 230. From left to right, insets: Doug Jones, Clem Thomas, Dil Johnson. Back row: George Bateman (trainer), Trevor Davies (committee), Wilf Jones, J.R. Davies, Len Blyth, Billy Williams, Dickie Dobbs, Glyn Rees, Leslie Davies (committee), Denny Hunt (committee). Middle row: Rowe Harding (committee), Graham Jeffreys, Dai Jones, Louis Fligelstone (committee), Bryn Evans (captain), Cliff Prosser (secretary), Alun Thomas, John Jenkins, Len Davies. Front row: Roy Sutton, Herbert Thomas, Ken Jones, Afan Daniel, Abel Thomas.

Above: This is the Swansea squad during pre-season training 1950. From left to right: Jock McKay, David Price, Alvn Bannister, Bernard Cajot, Billy Williams, Horace Phillips, Dickie Dobbs, Bryn Evans and Howard John.

Right: Swansea put up a splendid fight against the Springboks on 15 December 1951 before a crowd of nearly 40,000, but eventually were beaten by 11 points to 3 with a Dil Johnson try being Swansea's solitary score. The game remained even until the closing stages, and it was not until the last ten minutes that the tourists took control, scoring a try, conversion and penalty. Four of the players from the victorious Swansea team against the 1912 South Africans attended the game – Dai Williams, Harry Moulton, Edgar Morgan and Howell Lewis.

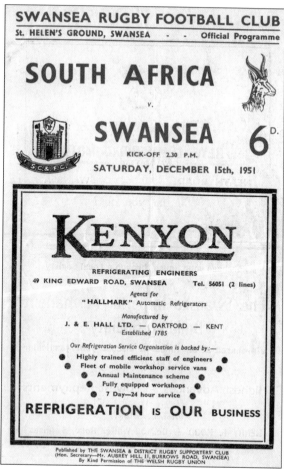

This is the Swansea team that played South Africa 1951. From left to right, back row: Tom Griffiths, 'Billy' Williams, Doug Jones, Harry Payne, Ken James, Clem Thomas, Perris James. Middle row: George Bateman (trainer), Roy Sutton, Dil Johnson, Len Blyth (captain), Horace Phillips, Brian Edwards, Terry Davies. Front row: Teifion Williams, Handel Greville.

Dil Johnson scores a try after 10 minutes to give Swansea a 3-0 lead against South Africa. Dil was a prolific try scorer who had the distinction of scoring a try for Swansea against three touring sides (1945 Kiwis, 1947 Australians and 1951 South Africans). He scored a total of 65 tries in 240 appearances for Swansea between 1945/46 and 1954/55, captaining the club in 1953/54. He gained a Wales cap versus England in 1953.

Above: It's smiles all round as the Swansea and South Africa players leave the field after a memorable game.

Right: Swansea took on the might of New Zealand on 12 December 1953 and rose to the occasion magnificently to secure an excellent 6-6 draw in front of a partisan 40,000 crowd. Yet another inexperienced youngster (following Haydn Tanner/Willie Davies in 1935) denied victory for New Zealand, on this occasion twenty-year-old centre John Faull, who kicked two long-distance penalties (both from about five yards inside his own half), in only his third game for Swansea.

This is the Swansea team v. New Zealand 1963. Back Row: John Faull, Jim Rees, Doug Jones, Len Blyth, Bruce Thomas, Bryan Jenkins, Horace Philips. Middle row: Wyn Bratton, Clem Thomas, Dil Johnson (captain), Billy Williams, Trevor Petherbridge, Teifion Williams. Front row: Goronwy Morgan, John Marker.

Scrum-half Goronwy Morgan finds space following a scrum to make a break. Right wing Teifion Williams (left of picture) waits in anticipation of a pass.

two

Pioneering
Tourists

The legendary Billy Bancroft congratulates Welsh winger, Ken Jones, on winning his 35th cap, equalling the record of Dicky Owen. The occasion was Wales versus Scotland at St Helen's in 1954, the last international to be staged on the ground until Tonga in 1997. In preparation for the England international in 1951 at St Helen's, Swansea Council moved the pitch 25 yards towards the town end. It was suggested as a result 75,000 could now be comfortably accommodated. As the 1954 game proved, however, regular international rugby was to become a thing of the past at St Helen's and the Council's aspirations were not to be.

This is a picture of the touring squad taken at Paddington station, London. Among the players is guest player Carwyn James (pictured fifth from the left, back row), who was later to gain 2 Wales caps from Llanelli and then become one of the game's all-time great coaches. Particularly remembered amongst his achievements are two victories against the mighty All Blacks – Llanelli in 1972 and the 1971 British Lions.

Right: Swansea became the first Western club to play behind the Iron Curtain with this tour of Rumania in August 1954. The first game marked the official opening of a stadium that was capable of accommodating 80,000 people and followed an invitation by the Rumanian Rugby Federation to Swansea because of their 'fame and tradition'. The Rumanian Minister of Sport said that the Swansea delegation had made a wonderful impression on all who had met them and were a credit to their club and country.

Below: Captain Clem Thomas leads out the Swansea team for their first game of the Rumanian tour. This was against the Locomotive club and was played in temperature above 100 degrees. This greatly affected Swansea who lost 23–12.

This is action from the game versus Locomotive on 21 August 1954. In the second game five days later, which was played in the evening and in cooler conditions, Swansea defeated Constructor by 16–5.

This represents an experienced front-row combination from the 1950s. Pictured from left to right are: Jim Rees, Trevor Petherbridge and W.O. 'Billy' Williams. Their club appearances amounted to 115, 152 and 304 respectively.

SWANSEA RUGBY FOOTBALL CLUB

St. HELEN'S GROUND, SWANSEA—Official Programme

RUMANIAN XV (BUCHAREST COMBINATION)

v.

SWANSEA

SATURDAY, SEPTEMBER 3rd, 1955

3D.

KICK-OFF 3.30 P.M.

The **SNAPPY CLEANERS**

Clean Beautifully

HIGH STREET (near Palace Theatre)

Published by THE SWANSEA & DISTRICT RUGBY SUPPORTERS' CLUB
Hon. Secretary—WILFRED E. HILL, 31 TRAFALGAR PLACE, BRYNMILL, SWANSEA

Right: Following Swansea's tour to Rumania at the start of the previous season, this reciprocal game represented the first visit to Wales by a side from behind the Iron Curtain. This game against a Rumanian XV, the first of the tour, took place on 3 September 1955 and Swansea were defeated by 19 points to 3 in front of 15,000 spectators, with an Alan Prosser Harries penalty their only points.

Below: The Rumanian players look to go on the attack against Swansea at St Helen's.

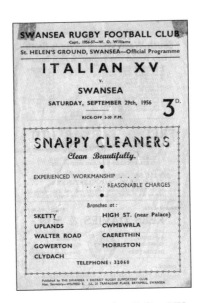

SWANSEA RUGBY FOOTBALL CLUB
Capt. 1956-57—W. O. Williams
St. HELEN'S GROUND, SWANSEA—Official Programme

GERMANY

v.

SWANSEA

THURSDAY, SEPTEMBER 6th, 1956

KICK-OFF 6.30 P.M.

3D.

SNAPPY CLEANERS
Clean Beautifully.
●
EXPERIENCED WORKMANSHIP . . . .
. . . . REASONABLE CHARGES
●

Branches at :

SKETTY   HIGH ST. (near Palace)
UPLANDS   CWMBWRLA
WALTER ROAD   CAEREITHIN
GOWERTON   MORRISTON
CLYDACH
                     TELEPHONE : 32060

Published by THE SWANSEA & DISTRICT RUGBY SUPPORTERS' CLUB
Hon. Secretary—WILFRED E. HILL, 31 TRAFALGAR PLACE, BRYNMILL, SWANSEA

SWANSEA RUGBY FOOTBALL CLUB
Capt. 1956-57—W. O. Williams
St. HELEN'S GROUND, SWANSEA—Official Programme

ITALIAN XV

v.

SWANSEA

SATURDAY, SEPTEMBER 29th, 1956

KICK-OFF 3-30 P.M.

3D.

SNAPPY CLEANERS
Clean Beautifully.
●
EXPERIENCED WORKMANSHIP . . . .
. . . . REASONABLE CHARGES
●

Branches at :

SKETTY   HIGH ST. (near Palace)
UPLANDS   CWMBWRLA
WALTER ROAD   CAEREITHIN
GOWERTON   MORRISTON
CLYDACH
                     TELEPHONE : 32060

Published by THE SWANSEA & DISTRICT RUGBY SUPPORTERS' CLUB
Hon. Secretary—WILFRED E. HILL, 31 TRAFALGAR PLACE, BRYNMILL, SWANSEA

In these games Germany were defeated 10-0 on 6 September 1956 and an Italian XV was beaten 13-5 on 29 September. This was the second occasion a German team was welcomed at St Helen's, as in the previous year the German youth team had played their first ever game in Wales there. This was also the first occasion an Italian XV played in Wales.

The Swansea squad prepare for their game against Padua, Italy. The club embarked on a three-game tour of Italy in May 1957. Swansea defeated Milan 6-0, lost 8-5 to Rome and beat Padua by 21 points to 9.

The 1957/58 squad with a playing record of: played 41, won 19, drawn 3, lost 19, points for 333, points against 322. From left to right, inset: Malcolm Rogers, Bryan Mullins, John Jeffries. Back row: Billy Williams, Gordon Morris, Islwyn Hopkins, Colin Johnson, Revd Ron Lloyd. Middle row: Len Blyth (match secretary), David Price (general secretary), Vivian Davies (committee), Len Davies, Gordon Lewis, Vernon Elias, Dudley Thomas, David Parkhouse, Roger Harding, Dickie Dobbs (trainer), Judge Rowe Harding (committee). Front row: Trevor Davies (committee), Alun Jones, Alan Prosser-Harries, Teifion Williams (captain), Clem Thomas, Haydn Pugh, Bruce Barter (committee).

The 1957/58 Athletic squad. From left to right, inset: R.L. Matthews, K.E. Pritchard. Back row: J. Morris, M. Jones, W. Alexander, D. John, B. O'Shea. Middle row: R.J. Pinney (trainer), J. Jeffreys, I. Jones, J.R. Davies, K. Jenkins, V. Elias, C. Hopkins (referee). Front row: R. Bolch, E. Burns, J. Llewellyn (captain), B. Harrop-Griffiths, Ivor Rees (committee), Brian Jones.

SWANSEA RUGBY FOOTBALL CLUB

Capt., 1957-58—Teifion Williams

St. HELEN'S GROUND, SWANSEA

OFFICIAL
SOUVENIR
PROGRAMME

6ᴰ

AUSTRALIA

Swansea
v.
Australia

SATURDAY, JANUARY 11th, 1958

KICK-OFF 2.30 P.M.

Published by THE SWANSEA & DISTRICT RUGBY SUPPORTERS' CLUB
Hon. Secretary—WILFRED E. HILL, 31 TRAFALGAR PLACE, BRYNMILL, SWANSEA

Left: Swansea were defeated by Australia 12 points to 6 on 11 January 1958 in front of a packed St Helen's crowd. In the lead-up to the game, Swansea received some good news with Billy Williams turning down an offer of £2,000 to go North. Swansea were unable to take advantage of playing with the wind and went in 12-0 down at the interval. A great second-half rally saw Swansea's pack dominate and Teifion Williams and Billy Williams score tries.

Below: Prop Billy Williams looks to release the ball, versus Australia, surrounded by fellow players (from left) John Faull, Islwyn Hopkins, Colin Johnson, Dudley Thomas and Haydn Pugh.

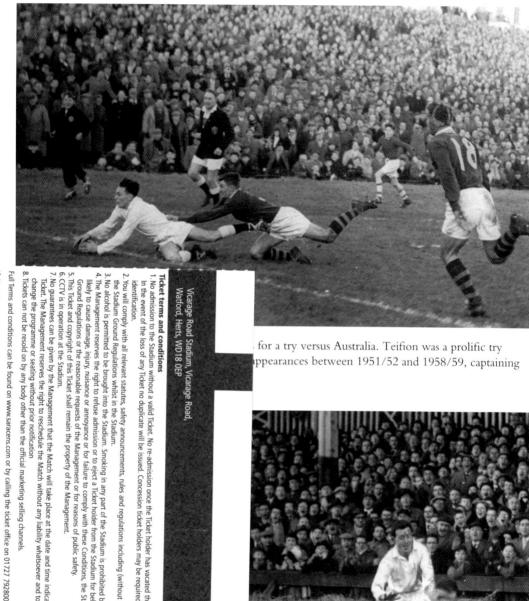

... for a try versus Australia. Teifion was a prolific try ... appearances between 1951/52 and 1958/59, captaining

... orner versus Australia with team-mate Bryan Mullins in

29

Clem Thomas played on 26 occasions for Wales as a flanker, scoring 1 try and captaining his country on 9 occasions. He toured South Africa with the British Lions in 1955, playing in 9 matches, including 2 international appearances. He also played 194 games for Swansea between 1947/48 and 1958/59, scoring 35 tries, captaining them in 1954/55. He also played for Cambridge University, Harlequins, London Welsh and Barbarians. After his distinguished playing career, he became a well-respected author, journalist and commentator on radio and television. He stood as a Liberal candidate at the 1974 general election and the 1979 European Parliamentary elections.

The official opening of the 'memorial gates' at the Gorse Lane end of the ground took place in December 1959. The gates were paid for by the supporters' club group and were dedicated by Canon H.C. Williams, Vicar of Swansea. In the picture (left to right) are Tom Davies, Mervyn Hosea, Eddie Rickard, Horace Leyshon, Cliff Bancroft, Aubrey Powell, Alan Lloyd, Albert Davies, Wilfred Hill and Dudley George.

Above: The 1960/61 squad, whose playing record was: played 45, won 25, drawn 5, lost 15, points for 482, points against 325. From left to right, back row: Haydn Mainwaring, Morrie Evans, Jim Clifford, Idwal Fisher, John Faull, John Jenkins, G.A. Burnett (committee). Middle row: Dai Jones (committee), Eifion Thomas, Mike Thomas, Gwyn Lewis, Billy Williams, Eiryn Lewis, Meirion Phillips, Dickie Dobbs (trainer). Front row: David Price (secretary), Roger Harding, Bryan Thomas, John Leleu (captain), Malcolm Rogers, Norman Gale, Len Blyth (committee).

Left: South Africa recorded a convincing 19 points to 3 win on 26 November 1960. Swansea's solitary points came from a Dewi Bebb try – the first scored against the Springboks on tour. Swansea, who had to play the entire second half with fourteen men after full-back Malcolm Rogers dislocated his elbow, put up a magnificent fight but the South Africans proved to be too strong.

31

Billy Williams, one of the finest prop forwards to ever wear a Swansea jersey, seen here demonstrating his footballing skills during the South Africa game, with team-mates Jim Clifford (left), Norman Gale and Morrie Evans watching in admiration.

Dewi Bebb sets off on a promising attack with plenty of close support from Swansea team-mates in the game versus South Africa.

Right: Prior to the South Africa game, Morlais Morris, a lifelong supporter of the club, had arranged for wood-carver Brinley Roberts of Swansea to produce an engraved shield to commemorate the event. The plaque, which depicts a springbok jumping over Swansea Castle and is made of Canadian maple, is inscribed with the names of all of the Swansea players who faced the South African touring team.

Below: Mayor Councillor F.C. Jenkins presents Mr Ferdie Bergh, manager of the 1960 South African touring team, with the wooden plaque. Also present at this ceremony are Mr Cliff Prosser (immediately left of the mayor), South African players and a number of Swansea club members and WRU officials.

Billy 'Stoker' Williams played on 22 occasions for Wales as a prop, scoring 2 tries. He toured South Africa with the British Lions in 1955, playing in 16 matches, including 4 international appearances. He also played 304 games for Swansea between 1949/50 and 1961/62, scoring 26 tries, captaining them in 1955/56 and 1956/57. He also played for Devonport Services, Royal Navy and the Barbarians.

Right: New Zealand recorded a 16 points to 9 victory on 14 December 1963, with Swansea's points coming from 2 penalties and a drop goal from full-back David Parkhouse. After 20 minutes New Zealand led 8-0 but Swansea led a brave fightback. In injury time New Zealand held a slender 11-9 lead and Swansea had hopes of success but a fourth try by the visitors sealed victory. The crowd, which was in excess of 30,000, would have witnessed a heroic Swansea performance that had come so close to victory.

Below: The Swansea team that played New Zealand in 1963. From left to right, back row: Glenn Barnes (coach), Geoff Thomas, Morrie Evans, Jim Clifford, Glan Morgan, Ron Jones, John Isaacs, Dickie Dobbs (trainer). Seated: Eiryn Lewis, Billy Upton, John Simonson, Dewi Bebb (captain), Warren Jenkins, David Parkhouse, Mike Thomas. Front row: Gareth Thomas, David Weaver.

SWANSEA RUGBY FOOTBALL CLUB

Capt. 1963-64—Dewi Bebb

ST. HELEN'S GROUND, SWANSEA — Souvenir Programme

SWANSEA
V
NEW ZEALAND

SATURDAY, DECEMBER 14th, 1963

KICK - OFF 2.30 P.M.

1/-

Jim Clifford leaps high to challenge for the line-out ball against the legendary Colin Meads. Jim made 216 appearances for the club between 1959/60 and 1966/67, scoring 9 tries. He also played for the Barbarians.

Dewi Bebb looks to start an attack with players in support.

SWANSEA RUGBY FOOTBALL CLUB

Captain 1964-65—DEWI BEBB

ST. HELEN'S GROUND, SWANSEA — Souvenir Programme **6**ᵈ·

1874 **90**ᵗʰ **1964**
ANNIVERSARY
CELEBRATION MATCH

SWANSEA

v.

INTERNATIONAL XV

THURSDAY, SEPTEMBER 3rd, 1964

KICK-OFF 6.30 P.M.

Published by THE SWANSEA & DISTRICT RUGBY SUPPORTERS' CLUB
Hon. Secretary—ARTHUR DAVIES, THE PHARMACY, YSGOL ST., ST. THOMAS, SWANSEA. Tel. 55353

Swansea defeated the International XV on 3 September 1964 by 22 points to 17, scoring 5 tries through Gareth Thomas (2), Tony Farthing, Mike Thomas and David Weaver with David Parkhouse adding a penalty and 2 conversions. The International XV comprised players from England, Ireland, Scotland and Wales. A month later Swansea began playing under their new floodlighting system.

Swansea gained a deserved victory over Australia by 9 points to 8 on 26 November 1966. Swansea's points came from a Mike Thomas try, a Brian Diment drop goal and a Stuart Ferguson penalty. This was the club's first win over a major touring side for thirty-one years and was the reward for three weeks of intensive training, when players turned up three nights a week to become match fit. By virtue of this victory, the 'All Whites' became recognized as the most successful Welsh club side against touring teams.

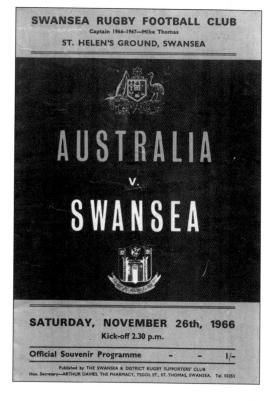

SWANSEA RUGBY FOOTBALL CLUB

Captain 1966-1967—Mike Thomas

ST. HELEN'S GROUND, SWANSEA

AUSTRALIA

v.

SWANSEA

SATURDAY, NOVEMBER 26th, 1966

Kick-off 2.30 p.m.

Official Souvenir Programme   -   -   1/-

Published by THE SWANSEA & DISTRICT RUGBY SUPPORTERS' CLUB
Hon. Secretary—ARTHUR DAVIES, THE PHARMACY, YSGOL ST., ST. THOMAS, SWANSEA. Tel. 55353

The Swansea team that defeated Australia. From left to right, back row: David Weaver, Geoff Atherton, Byron Mainwaring, Jim Clifford, Dai Davies, Dewi Bebb, Stuart Ferguson. Middle row: Roy Thomas, Doug Jones, Stuart Davies, Mike Thomas (captain), Morrie Evans, Brian Diment. Front row: John Davies, Clive Rowlands.

Mike Thomas scores a try for Swansea with Geoff Atherton (number 6) celebrating. Mike made 320 appearances for the club between 1960/61 and 1968/69, scoring 71 tries. He also captained the club in 1966/67.

Ken Catchpole challenged by Clive Rowlands (right) and Geoff Atherton (left). Former Wales captain Clive Rowlands OBE, was a larger-than-life character, who had led Wales to a Triple Crown in 1965 and went on to coach Wales, became a Welsh selector and was manager of various Wales tours and the British Lions to Australia in 1989. He was president of the WRU in 1989. He made 84 appearances for the club between 1965/66 and 1967/68, scoring 26 points (5 tries, 1 drop goal and 4 conversions), captaining the club in 1967/68.

Dewi Bebb played on 34 occasions for Wales as a wing, scoring 11 tries. He toured South Africa with the British Lions in 1962, playing in 8 matches, including 2 international appearances. He also toured in 1966 to Australia and New Zealand, gaining 6 international appearances, and ending the tour as joint leading try scorer with Mike Gibson. He also played 221 games for Swansea between 1958/59 and 1966/67, scoring 87 tries, and captaining them in 1963/64 and 1964/65. He also played for Royal Navy and Barbarians. After his distinguished playing career, he worked in the media, principally with HTV.

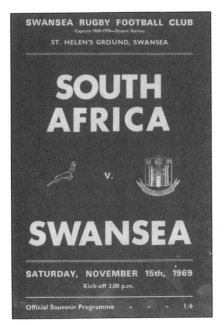

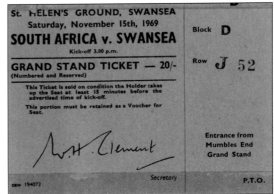

Above, and above right: South Africa defeated Swansea by 12 points to nil on 15 November 1969 in front of 20,000 spectators. This was only the second occasion that Swansea had failed to score against a major touring team; the first instance being against the Maoris in 1888 when the score was 11-0. All South Africa's points were scored with the wind in the first half, coming from 3 penalties and a try.

Right: This leaflet issued by the Swansea anti-apartheid committee was distributed around the vicinity of St Helen's leading up to and during the day of the game against South Africa. For the first time in its long and distinguished history, St Helen's witnessed a substantial police presence. The remaining Springbok matches in Wales were made admission by ticket only and no tickets were sold on the day of the match.

STOP THE BOKS

THE SPRINGBOK TEAM does not represent South Africa. They were not chosen from all sportsmen in South Africa. They represent only the APARTHEID system which does not allow whites and non-whites to play together, and inflicts every inhumanity on non-whites. 81% of the population are non-white yet only one in fifteen of the sports fields in S. Africa are for use by non-whites, who even require a permit to watch matches.

Many S. African sportsmen wishing to compete internationally have been forced, because of their race, to leave the country. Many sportsmen here of international standing cannot compete in S. Africa against a national team and cannot use the same facilities-even lavatories-as whites. Among these are such names as Basil D'Olivera, Gary Sobers and Frank Wilson.

The Springboks Rugby Tour of this country is just as much an intrusion of the Apartheid political system as the D'Olivera Affair of last year. BY WELCOMING THEM, PLAYING AGAINST THEM, GOING TO THEIR MATCHES, WE ARE ACCEPTING THEIR EVIL POLITICS.

Opponents of Apartheid in S. Africa want the 'Boks stopped- NOW AND IN THE FUTURE. If they are stopped those who support Apartheid will realise as never before that they and their policies are rejected.

JOIN THOSE, LIKE JOHN TAYLOR, WELSH INTERNATIONAL, WHO REJECT APARTHEID IN SPORT. JOIN US ON THE 15th!

Boycott the Match - Join the Protest

GATHER OUTSIDE GUILDHALL FROM 12 am. NOVEMBER 15

BEFORE MARCH TO ST. HELENS.

Issued by Swansea Anti-Apartheid Committee

Above: This is the Swansea squad versus South Africa 1969. From left to right, back row: Morrie Evans (coach), David Winslett, David Morgan, Malcolm Henwood, Mike James, John Joseph, Roger Hyndman, Mel James, John Davies, Roy Thomas, David Bowen, Eddie Rickard (trainer). Front row: Alan Rutherford, Tom Pullman, Hylton Bowen, Clive Dyer, Stuart Davies (captain), Stuart Ferguson, Lyndon Jones, Phil Bessant.

Left and above: The heavy police presence all around St Helen's can be evidenced from these photographs, which resemble more a football game. The most amazing scenes in the history of Welsh rugby occurred at this event. Shortly after half time, between thirty and forty anti-apartheid demonstrators burst on to the field to stage a sit down protest at the South African visit. Police and stewards cleared the field in five minutes. Ten policemen were treated in hospital for injuries sustained as a result of the protests. The match led to protracted enquiries by 'outside' police forces and the Home Office Inspectorate.

This is the Swansea Schools' under-11 squad that became the inaugural D.C. Thomas Cup winners in 1969/70. From left to right, back row: Ron Perkins, David Matthews, Geoff Quick, Charlie Boyd, Geraint Williams, Bill Sterio, Eric Thomas, Danny Davies, Roy Bennett, Clem Williams. Boys standing: G. Stock, K. Davies, D. Sims, M. Gorecki, S. Morris, R. Huxtable, D. Jenkins, S. Jenvey. Seated: J. O'Kolo, S. Morris, A. Lamnea, Alan Williams, L. Crook (captain), J. Trotman, D. Newman. Front row: C. Newell, M. Charles, R. Evans, A. Watts, D. Cook, K. Evans, P. Rees, S. Cook.

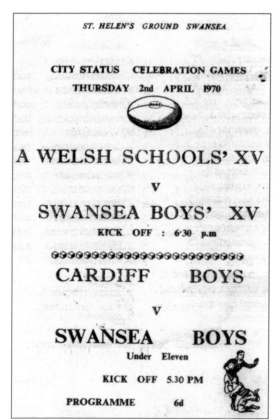

Two schoolboy games were organized for 2 April 1970 to celebrate Swansea's newly-acquired city status. These games were played at St Helen's and involved an under-11s clash between Swansea and Cardiff, and a Welsh schools' XV against a Swansea boys' XV.

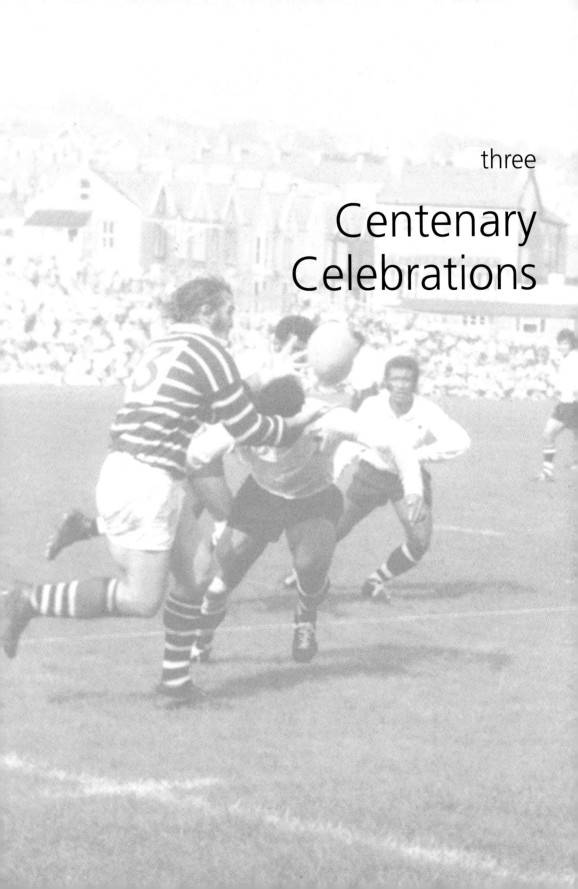

three

Centenary
Celebrations

Swansea's international artist Andrew Vicari designed the osprey depicted on the left. Although it does not feature on the official club crest, the osprey appeared on the City Council's coat of arms and was used by the club as a symbol for their centenary season. The osprey was chosen because of its speed, grace, commitment and beauty in flight – a pictorial metaphor for Swansea's brand of rugby. The osprey was later to feature on the crest of the Neath/Swansea regional team that was established in 2003.

The club enjoyed its most successful post war season to date in 1973/74, winning the Merit Table, with the playing record of: played 47, won 31, drawn 4, lost 12, points for 728, points against 451.

Vivian Davies initially played for Swansea then Gloucester before returning to Swansea. He was a scrum-half who made a total of 41 appearances for the first team between 1947/48 and 1955/56 and also played for and captained the Athletic team. He was selected for the Welsh trial in 1952/53. After his playing days were over he initially joined the committee and then became fixture secretary from 1958/59. He was club chairman for five consecutive seasons from 1972/73, including the 1973/74 centenary season. He later became club president and is currently life patron. His father, Trevor Davies, was also a former player and on the committee and chairman.

The Swansea and Fiji teams for their encounter on 8 September 1973, a game the tourists won overwhelmingly by 31 points to nil. The large crowd was very appreciative of the flowing rugby of the islanders in what was the first occasion Swansea had played them.

The Swansea players look to launch an attack against Fiji at St Helen's.

Swansea Cricket & Football Club
CENTENARY YEAR
1874 - 1974

DINNER

to

Fijian Touring Team

Dragon Hotel, Swansea.
Saturday 8th September, 1973

In The Chair
T. J. Vivian Davies
(Chairman Swansea Cricket & Football Club)

Swansea Cricket and Football Club

Centenary Banquet

1874 — 1974

College House, University College, Swansea
Thursday, 18th April 1974   7.00 p.m. for 7.30 p.m.

TICKET £5·50
Complimentary
Dress formal

Amongst the club's centenary celebrations was a dinner in honour of the Fijian touring team on the evening of the game (8 September 1973) and a centenary banquet at the University College, Swansea on 18 April 1974.

The 1973/74 centenary squad. From left to right, back row: Dickie Dobbs (linesman), Roger Hyndman, Barry Clegg, Geoff Wheel, Roger Blyth, Phil Llewellyn, Peter Thomas, Gerwyn Jones, Jim Trott (trainer). Middle row: Mike Yandle, Mervyn Davies, Robert Dyer (captain), Ieuan Evans (coach), Darrel Cole, Alan Mages. Front row: Gwynfor Higgins, David Protheroe, Trevor Evans.

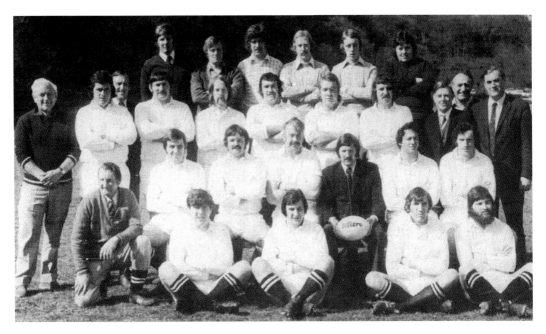

This is the Swansea Athletic squad in the 1973/74 centenary season, under the captaincy of Stuart Davies.

This is Swansea's youth squad of 1973/74. From left to right, back row: Leonard Miller, G. Killa, R. Lewis, P. Arnold, J. Davies, D. Thomas, C. Rees, C. Presley. Seated: T. John, I. Hopkins, A. Daniel, G. Nutt (captain), D. James, J. Richards, S. Ellesworthy.

ST. HELEN'S
GROUND, SWANSEA

Australia

Swansea

SATURDAY, 3rd
NOVEMBER, 1973

Kick-Off 2.30 p.m.

SOUVENIR CENTENARY
PROGRAMME — TEN PENCE
(Donation to Club)

Swansea achieved a 9-9 draw against Australia on 3 November 1973, with their points coming from a Mike Yandle try and a penalty and conversion by Roger Blyth. In front of a 15,000 crowd, Swansea were leading 9-6 three minutes into injury time, when they transgressed offside and Australia scored their third penalty to secure the draw.

Mike Yandle crosses the line to score near the posts. This was followed by a Roger Blyth conversion. Mike scored 3 tries for the club in 30 appearances between 1973/74 and 1974/75.

St. Helen's Ground, Swansea

Welsh Rugby Union President's XV

versus

Swansea

Wednesday, 10th April, 1974

Kick-Off 7.00 p.m.

Programme 5p (Donation to Club)

Left: A special centenary celebration game took place on 10 April 1974 against a WRU President's XV. Swansea won emphatically by 50 points to 9, with tries by Roger Blyth (3), Gwynfor Higgins (2), Roger Hyndman, Mike James, Gerwyn Jones and Alan Mages. Roger Blyth (5) and Robert Dyer (2) added the conversions. The President's XV comprised players from other Welsh clubs. This was the last of the club's special centenary fixtures.

Below: The Swansea squad is put through their paces by coach Ieuan Evans in pre-season training, in preparation for the 1974/75 season. Ieuan had been a former Swansea player who made a total of 7 appearances between 1946/47 and 1951/52. He had been coach at Llanelli and Florence University (Italy) before taking on the same role at Swansea in 1970, becoming the fifth coach in as many years. He brought much-needed confidence and team spirit to the dressing room and was instrumental in streamlining the number of selectors from seven to three. He resigned at the end of the 1974/75 season and later became vice president and then president of the WRU and chair of the WRU coaching committee. He had for many seasons coached the Welsh Youth XV.

Australia secured a 12 points to 6 victory on 29 November 1975 in front of 20,000 spectators, with Swansea's points coming from two John Rees penalties. Australia were leading 9-6 when Swansea prop Phil Llewellyn had a potentially match–winning try disallowed. Australia scored a penalty in injury time to secure the win. Australian wing Paddy Batch was sent off for a dangerous tackle 14 minutes into the second half – the first occasion an Australian tourist was ordered to the dressing room since 1947.

Swansea and Australia forwards set off in pursuit of the loose ball during their tussle at St Helen's.

WELSH RUGBY UNION

W.R.U. CHALLENGE CUP
Semi-Final

PONTYPOOL
v.
SWANSEA

SUNDAY, 28th MARCH, 1976
CARDIFF R.F.C. GROUND
CARDIFF ARMS PARK

K.O. 3 p.m.   Programme 10p

W.R.U. Challenge Cup
Semi-Final

PONTYPOOL v. SWANSEA
CARDIFF ARMS PARK
SUNDAY, 28th MARCH, 1976
KICK OFF 3 p.m.

SOUTH STAND
Quay Street Entrance   № 033

TICKET
1.25

This cup semi-final will be forever remembered as the game at which Mervyn Davies suffered a brain haemorrhage that ended his career prematurely at twenty-nine years of age. Mervyn collapsed during a period of open play and was carried off on a stretcher, but happily recovered to lead a normal life. Swansea won the game 22-14, despite prop Alan Lewis having to leave the field injured, which resulted in flanker Baden Evans being forced to play as prop forward.

This is the Swansea team that defeated Pontypool in the cup semi-final. From left to right, standing: Stan Addicott (coach), John Evans, Mark Keyworth, Trevor Evans, Alan Lewis, Geoff Wheel, Barry Clegg, Phil Llewellyn, John Rees, Roger Blyth, Baden Evans, Alan Meredith, Bernard Cajot (trainer). Seated: David Richards, Roy Woodward, Mervyn Davies (captain), Alan Mages, Gerwyn Jones, Roger Davies.

Mervyn Davies played on 38 occasions for Wales, scoring 2 tries and featured in 3 Triple Crown and 2 Grand Slam sides. He played on 2 British Lions tours, in 1971 to Australia and New Zealand and 1974 to South Africa, making a total of 8 international appearances. He played 88 games for Swansea scoring 15 tries, having joined from London Welsh in 1972. He captained Wales in his last 9 international appearances and Swansea in 1975/76, his last season. At the time of his premature retirement from the game, he was favourite to captain the 1977 British Lions. He also played for Barbarians. He was Welsh Rugby Player of the Year on two occasions, in 1975 and 1976. His trademarks were a bristling bandit-style moustache and the broad swathe of white bandage that protected his ears. His father had also played for Swansea and appeared in a Victory International match in 1946.

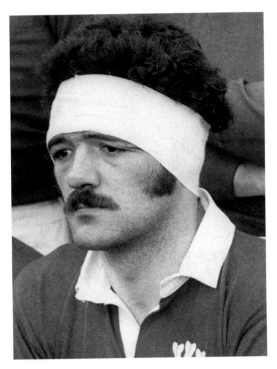

Swansea Schools undertook a seventy-fifth anniversary New Zealand tour in 1976. From left to right, back row: John Adams, Malcolm Dacey, Paul Howells, Russell Hayward, Ken Isaac, Eric Jenkins, Lionel Solly, Paul Bennett, David Fox. Middle row: Russell Huxtable, David Jenkins, Nigel Mason, Jeffrey Evans, Gareth John, David Rennie, Michael Tucker, Graham Stock, Mark Gibbs. Front row: Martin Lloyd, Gareth Williams, Gerald Lindenburn (assistant manager), Gareth Roberts (captain), Horace Phillips (manager), Leighton Crook, Gareth Evans (coach), Keith Evans, Anthony Wallis.

These are the Swansea under-13, under-14 and under-16 teams and officials in a happy mood before leaving on a tour of Hampshire in 1977.

This is action from the Barbarians clash on 27 March 1978 in a game that Swansea won by 36 points to 15. In the picture Bill Beaumont is surrounded by four Swansea players, from left to right: Phil Llewellyn, Geoff Wheel, Barry Clegg and Mark Keyworth.

Trevor Evans played on 10 occasions for Wales as a flanker, scoring 2 tries. He played 242 games for Swansea between 1970/71 and 1978/79, scoring 37 tries, and captained the club in 1976/77. He also toured with the British Lions in 1977 to New Zealand, playing 13 games, including a single international appearance. He also played for Wales B and Barbarians.

Phil Llewellyn (centre of picture) played on 5 occasions for Wales as a prop. He played 430 games for Swansea between 1966/67 and 1980/81, scoring 42 tries, and captained the club in 1971/72. He toured Canada twice, with Wales in 1973 and with the Barbarians in 1976. He has the third most club appearances post-war, behind Richard Moriarty (472) and Keith Colclough (431). Phil is pictured here with internationals Geoff Wheel (left) and future club player Maurice Colclough (right).

four

Sch.....
Cup Success

SCHWEPPES
WELSH RUGBY UNION

CUP FINAL

NEWPORT v SWANSEA

Saturday 29th April 1978

Kick-off
3 p.m.
THE CARDIFF
ARMS PARK

SECRETARY W.R.U.   OFFICIAL PROGRAMME 25p

Left and above: Swansea won the Schweppes Welsh Cup for the first time, defeating Newport by 13 points to 9 in the final at the National Stadium, on 29 April 1978. A crowd of nearly 40,000 paid a record £80,000 to witness the event. Swansea's points came from a Jeff Herdman try, drop goals by David Richards and Gareth Jenkins and a Roger Blyth penalty. David Richards won the man-of-the-match award. This proved to be a momentous day for the City of Swansea as the football club also secured promotion.

Right: This is the 1978 cup final Swansea rosette. It very nearly wasn't to be. In a preliminary round at Burry Port, the final score was 6-6. In extra time, the home side went into the lead 9-6 following a penalty by former All White Dennis Lewis. Two late tries by Roger Davies and Gareth Jenkins eventually resulted in a 19-9 Swansea win.

Below: This is Swansea's cup final winning team of 1978. From left to right, back row: Clive Norling (referee), Roger Blyth, Peter Thomas, Alan Mages, Phil Jones, Richard Moriarty, Barry Clegg, Phil Llewellyn, Huw Rees, Mark Keyworth, Trevor Evans, Cennydd Thomas (touch judge). Middle row: Corris Thomas (touch judge), Gerwyn Jones, Alun Donovan, David Richards, Geoff Wheel, Alan Meredith (captain), Jeff Herdman, David James, Huw Davies, Hywel Hopkins. Front row: Gareth Jenkins, Roy Woodward.

Above: Here Jeff Herdman completes a ten-metre dash for the only try of the game after Phil Llewellyn had secured short-line possession to set up the try. Jeff played 257 games for the club between 1971/72 and 1983/84, scoring 62 tries. He also played for Wales B and Barbarians.

Right: Swansea captain Alan Meredith holds the WRU cup aloft at the National Stadium after the club's victory over Newport. Alan played a total of 197 games for Swansea between 1971/72 and 1981/82, scoring 65 tries. He was to captain the team for a second successive season in 1978/79 following this cup success and also played for the Barbarians.

The club won the WRU National Sevens title for the first time in 1979. In so doing, they achieved a record margin win in the final, 42-6 versus Llanelli. On the way to the final, Swansea defeated Burry Port 32-6, Haverfordwest 30-0 and Cardiff College of Education 12-10 (winning with the last kick of the match in what was a tense semi-final). Captain Jeff Herdman was selected as the player of the tournament. From left to right, back row: Phil Llewellyn, David Richards, Mike Langdon, Jeff Davies. Seated: Gareth Jenkins, Jeff Herdman (captain), Stan Addicott (coach), Huw Davies. Stan Addicott had taken over as coach in 1975/76 and continued until Ian Hall took over in 1982/83. This represented the most successful post-war period up to that date with the club winning the cup in 1978 and becoming a championship-winning team in 1979/80 and 1980/81.

This is the Swansea squad under the management of Gordon Morris prior to departure on their tour of the Far East in August 1979. All four games were won by a comfortable margin, a Thai National XV was beaten 68 points to 6, Royal Bangkok Sports Club 48-12, Selangor Sports Club (Kuala Lumpur) 74-6 and the British Forces Hong Kong 46-3.

five

Anglo Welsh Champions

Among the 1979/80 season's achievements the team were Western Mail champions, *Sunday Telegraph* and *Daily Mail* Anglo-Welsh champions and *Sunday Telegraph* Team of the Season. In addition the team exceeded 1,000 points in a season for the first time, Tony Swift's 29 tries were a post-war season's best, David Richards was chosen as Welsh Rugby Player of the Year and David Richards and Clive Williams were chosen to tour with the British Lions to South Africa. From left to right, back row: Mike James (selector), Dickie Dobbs (linesman), Mark Wyatt, Keith Colclough, Clive Williams, Trevor Cheeseman, Barry Clegg, Richard Moriarty, Mark Davies, Mark Keyworth, Roger Blyth, Hywel Hopkins, Bernard Cajot (trainer), Gordon Morris (chairman of selectors), Lemmuel Evans (selector). Middle row: Eddie Rickard (baggage master), Jeff Herdman, Tony Swift, Stan Addicott (coach), Geoff Wheel (captain), John Llewellyn (chairman), David Richards, Alun Donovan. Front row: Roy Lewis, Alan Meredith, Brynmor Williams, Huw Davies, Malcolm Dacey.

Welsh Brewers LTD

1980

Celebration Dinner

to honour

SWANSEA R.F.C.

"WESTERN MAIL"
WELSH CLUB CHAMPIONS

and

"The Welsh Player of the Year"

Elected by the Welsh Rugby Writers Association

at

THE BINDLES BANQUETING SUITE
THE KNAP, BARRY

Friday, 11th July

A celebration dinner took place in Barry on 11 July 1980 to honour the club as Western Mail Welsh club champions for the 1979/80 season, this being the club's first championship triumph since 1912/13. The club's overall playing record in 1979/80 was: played 46, won 40, drawn 1, lost 5, points for 1,196 and points against 384. With the success that followed in the next few seasons, this represented a second 'golden era' for the club.

Swansea won the WRU National Sevens for a second successive season, defeating Newport 16-12 in the final. Captain Jeff Herdman scored the decisive try in extra time and retained the Player of the Tournament award he won the previous season. Swansea reached the final with victories over Tenby 24-0, Tumble 16-4 and Aberavon 32-0. From left to right, standing: Jeff Davies, Roy Lewis, Neil Edwards, Mark Wyatt. Kneeling: Gareth Jenkins, Jeff Herdman (captain), Trevor Cheeseman.

St. Helen's Ground
Swansea

Swansea

New Zealand

Left: Swansea were comprehensively defeated by New Zealand 32-0 on 25 October 1980 in front of a 25,000 crowd. Despite this reverse, 1980/81 was yet another successful season, the overall playing record being: played 47, won 41, drawn 1, lost 5, points for 1,242, points against 399. Among the season's achievements the club were Merit Table winners, the *Sunday Telegraph* Team of the Season for the second consecutive season and had managed a record season's points total.

Below: Here the New Zealand team performs the traditional Haka (the generic term for Maori dance). This pre-match ritual involves slapping the hands against the thighs, puffing out the chest, bending the knees and stamping of the feet.

In anticipation of the large attendance, the club erected this temporary stand at the town end of the ground to accommodate the extra supporters.

Alan Meredith sets off on a run here, having broken through the New Zealand defence. In the background are fellow All Whites Malcolm Dacey, Gareth Jenkins and David Richards. Alan acquired the distinction of having played for the club in every position in the back division, from scrum half to full back.

This is the 1980/81 First XV squad. From left to right, back row: Gordon Morris (chairman, match committee), Dudley Thomas (match secretary), Dickie Dobbs (committee and touch judge), Clive Williams, Mike Ruddock, Gareth John, Arthur Emyr, Mark Wyatt, Richard Moriarty, Barry Clegg, Roger Blyth, Hywel Hopkins, Steve Davies, Alun Donovan, Mike James (match committee), Lemmuel Evans (match committee). Middle row: Gareth Jenkins, Tony Swift, David Richards, Geoff Wheel (captain), Stan Addicott (coach), Jeff Herdman, Trevor Cheeseman, Keith Williams, Eddie Rickard (attendant), Bernard Cajot (trainer). Front row: Huw Rees, David Thomas, Brynmor Williams, Mark Davies, Huw Davies, Malcolm Dacey.

The All Whites former players' association was established in 1981 and continues up to the present day. The original committee was selected at the inaugural meeting and comprised Len Blyth (chairman), Norman Blyth, David Bowen, Bryn Evans (secretary), Gwyn Griffiths, Harry Jenkins, Dil Johnson (treasurer), Dai Jones, Gilbert Jones, Harry Payne and Vernon Rees Davies.

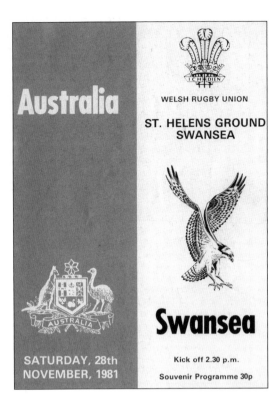

Australia

WELSH RUGBY UNION

ST. HELENS GROUND SWANSEA

Swansea

SATURDAY, 28th NOVEMBER, 1981

Kick off 2.30 p.m.

Souvenir Programme 30p

Left: Australia secured a 12 points to 3 victory on 28 November 1981 with Swansea's points coming from a Malcolm Dacey drop goal. Going into the third quarter, Swansea held a slender 3-0 lead, but both Mike Ruddock and Barry Clegg went off injured and after that Australia scored 3 tries. A week earlier against South Wales Police in the cup, both Tony Swift and David Richards had pulled hamstrings to rule them out of the clash with the tourists.

Below: Trevor Cheeseman looks to offload the ball to Mike Ruddock during the Australia game. Trevor made a total of 287 appearances for the club between 1975/76 and 1986/87, scoring 20 tries. He was a utility forward, playing regularly in both the second and back rows. He also played for England at under-23 level.

Right: Richard Moriarty in action against Australia in 1981 – before the introduction of new lineout laws! For this game he partnered Barry Clegg in the second row. In his long and distinguished career for Swansea and Wales, Dicky demonstrated his versatility by playing as a second row (front and middle-line jumper), number eight and blind-side flanker.

Below: Pictured here are the Swansea schoolboys under-15 squad, 1981/82. Two future British Lions are featured, namely captain Richard Webster (with ball) and Anthony Clement (front row, right).

Swansea Cricket & Football Club

ZIMBABWE TOUR 1982

Left: After a relatively successful 1981/82 season: played 43, won 32, drawn 1, lost 10, points for 1,082 and points against 446, the club embarked on an end-of-season tour to Zimbabwe. After wins against Matabeleland (26-19), Zimbabwe (28-6) and Mashonoland (23-22), the team lost narrowly 31-30 in their second fixture against Zimbabwe. The manager of the touring party was Vivian Davies.

Below: The Swansea squad, winners of the Snelling Sevens, August 1982. Arthur Emyr replaced Tony Swift for the finals. Hooker Jeff Herdman won the Bill Everson award as the outstanding player of the tournament. From left to right, back row: Ian Hall (coach), Mark Wyatt, Arthur Emyr, Mike Ruddock, Steve Davies. Front row: Trevor Cheeseman, Huw Rees, David Richards (captain), Jeff Herdman, Paul Gallagher. Swansea also went on to win the Snelling Sevens in 1989 and 1991 and won the Worthington Sevens in 1995.

Right: Geoff Wheel played on 32 occasions for Wales as a second row. He played 318 games for Swansea between 1970/71 and 1982/83, scoring 24 tries and captaining the club in 1979/80 and 1980/81. He was a fine scrummager, but his most important contribution was in the maul, often presenting the scrum half with unlikely ball. He was originally chosen for the 1977 Lions tour but was subsequently withdrawn on medical advice just prior to departure. He has the dubious honour of being the first Wales player to be sent off in an international match (*v* Ireland 1977). He also played for Wales B and Barbarians. In his earlier days, he had played football for Swansea City reserves.

Below: This photograph shows the New Zealand Maoris performing their traditional Haka before the game on 30 October 1982. All fifteen players have simultaneously leapt off the ground at this precise moment in time.

The successful 1982/83 squad. From left to right, back row: Lemmuel Evans (match committee), Dickie Dobbs (linesman), Stuart Evans, Gareth Roberts, Clive Williams, Mike Ruddock, Barry Clegg, Gareth John, Malcolm Dacey, Huw Gilson, Gareth Jenkins, Roger Blyth, Bernard Cajot (trainer), Mike James (chairman, selection committee). Front row: Trevor Cheeseman, Tony Swift, Huw Davies, Jeff Herdman, Ian Hall (coach), David Richards (captain), Norman Blyth (chairman), Mark Davies, Paul Gallagher, Mark Wyatt, Kevin Hopkins, Keith Colclough, Arthur Emyr, Eddie Rickard (baggage master).

Captain David Richards being presented with the Merit Table trophy. In yet another successful season, the overall playing record was: played 47, won 40, lost 7, points for 1,131, points against 576. Among the season's achievements the club were Merit Table winners, *Western Mail* champions, *Daily Mail* Anglo-Welsh champions for the second occasion in four seasons and the *Sunday Telegraph* team of the season for the third occasion in four seasons.

Right: Australia defeated Swansea by 17 points to 7 on 30 October 1984, Swansea's points coming from an Arthur Emyr try and a Mark Wyatt penalty. With 14 minutes of the game remaining, a 400-amp fuse blew in the lighting, which brought a premature (and dark) end to the proceedings. Prior to the game, Swansea had been hoping for a repeat of the famous 1935 win versus New Zealand when it was teenage half backs Willie Davies and Haydn Tanner who were chiefly responsible for the 11–3 win. It was now the turn of another pair of teenage half backs, Aled Williams and Robert Jones, but unfortunately it was not to be.

Below: The steam rises at a scrum before the lights went out versus Australia.

Welsh Rugby Union
St. Helen's Ground
Swansea

AUSTRALIA

SWANSEA

**Tuesday
October 30th 1984**
Kick-Off 7.00 p.m.

PROGRAMME 50p
(Donation to Club)

The club embarked on a single game tour of Italy and played a Colonna XV on 1 June 1985. The match, which Swansea won by 27 points to 14, had been at the instigation of Professor Herbert Beynon and was arranged in order to assist an Italian association against leukaemia disease. Silvio Lisato, president of the organizing committee welcomed Swansea thus: 'your participation honours Italian rugby and all its supporters and fans… As far as rugby is concerned, you are the most authentic and qualified representatives.'

Roger Blyth played as a full back/centre on 6 occasions for Wales, scoring 1 try and 1 conversion. He made a total of 395 club appearances between 1968/69 and 1988/89. His club career points total of 2,412 (127 tries, 340 penalties, 12 drop goals and 431 conversions) is the second highest behind Mark Wyatt. He also played for Wales B and Barbarians. He has been one of the main benefactors associated with the club since the advent of professionalism. He is the son of Len and nephew of Norman Blyth and Alun Thomas – all former All Whites.

This is the Swansea team that faced Fiji on 16 October 1985. From left to right, back row: Byron Mugford, Stuart Davies, Keith Colclough, Trevor Cheeseman, Maurice Colclough, Richard Moriarty, John Williams, Mark Thomas, Ian Jeffries, Huw Gilson, Clive Williams, Mike James, Stuart Davies. Seated: Stuart Evans, Mark Titley, Malcolm Dacey, Gwyn Lewis, Mark Davies (captain), Jeff Herdman, David Richards, Kevin Hopkins, Huw Davies, Bernard Cajot. Front row: Keith Williams, Paul Hitchings, Aled Williams, Dominic Setaro.

Malcolm Dacey looks to set up an attack, supported by Keith (left) and Maurice (right) Colclough versus Fiji. Swansea lost the game 23 points to 14, with their points coming from tries by Malcolm Dacey and David Richards and 2 Kevin Hopkins penalties.

Above: David Richards played on 17 occasions for Wales as a centre or wing, scoring 4 tries. He played 305 games for Swansea between 1972/73 and 1985/86, scoring 111 tries, and captained the club in 1981/82, 1982/83 and 1983/84. He toured with the 1980 British Lions to South Africa, playing 7 games, including 1 international appearance. He was a reserve for the 1977 British Lions tour to New Zealand, and he was Welsh Rugby Player of the Year in 1980. He also played for Wales B and Barbarians. After his playing career he became a National selector.

Right: The club undertook an end of season tour to Zimbabwe and Kenya in May 1987. During a break between the 6 matches played the club visited Victoria Falls on 20 May. After an initial 19-19 draw against Goshawks, Swansea won their remaining 5 games, including a 40-15 victory over Kenya. Former player Gwyn Lewis was manager of the tour party.

The three progarmmes from the Snelling Sevens tournament that Swansea were victorious in: 1982, 1989 and 1991.

Swansea visited Dunvant in celebration of the latter's centenary season in 1987. On this occasion, Dunvant won by 19 points to 16 with Swansea's scores coming from tries by Ian Davies, Arthur Emyr and David Jones and 2 conversions from Adrian Stewart. Swansea regularly played at the 'smaller' clubs in special commemorative fixtures that were a boost to the home teams' finances. It was also an opportunity for Swansea to express its gratitude for providing it with players from such teams throughout the club's long and distinguished history.

Dunvant Rugby Football Club

(Affiliated to the Welsh Rugby Union)

Centenary 1887-1987

DUNVANT

V
SWANSEA

Wednesday October 21st 1987 KO 7.00 pm

Broadacre Dunvant

Admission £1.00   OAP/children 50p

Swansea had a total of eight players representing Wales at the inaugural World Cup in 1987, including the captain Richard Moriarty. From left to right, top row: Richard Moriarty, Kevin Hopkins, Malcolm Dacey, Robert Jones, Paul Moriarty. Bottom row: Mark Titley (replacement), Richard Webster (replacement), David Young (replacement).

Swansea were defeated in their first WRU Cup game of the 1988/89 season at the last sixty-four stage of the competition. The 18-8 shock defeat came at Glamorgan Wanderers on 19 November 1988, with the Moriarty brothers registering Swansea's points with a try apiece. Here, Paul Moriarty attempts to claim the ball with Robert Lakin about to pounce for Glamorgan Wanderers.

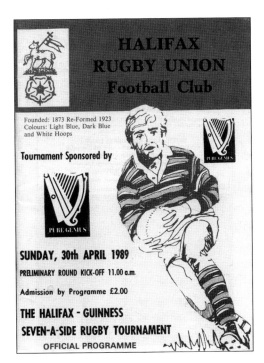

HALIFAX RUGBY UNION Football Club

Founded: 1873 Re-Formed 1923
Colours: Light Blue, Dark Blue and White Hoops

Tournament Sponsored by

PURE GENIUS

SUNDAY, 30th APRIL 1989

PRELIMINARY ROUND KICK-OFF 11.00 a.m.

Admission by Programme £2.00

THE HALIFAX - GUINNESS
SEVEN-A-SIDE RUGBY TOURNAMENT
OFFICIAL PROGRAMME

On Sunday 30 April 1989 Swansea took part in the third annual Halifax Guinness seven-a-side tournament. Twenty clubs took part representing England, Ireland, Scotland and Wales with Swansea being one of the eight seeded teams. Swansea went on to win the competition (and with it the cup and £1,000 prize money) by defeating Alnwick 34-0, Jedforest 22-0, Ards 18-12 and Richmond 23-16 in the final.

Anthony Clement (left) in action with Malcolm Dacey. Malcolm played on 15 occasions for Wales as an outside half, scoring 7 penalties, 3 drop goals and a conversion. He played 263 games for Swansea between 1978/79 and 1991/92, scoring 46 tries. He was also a British Lion by virtue of coming on as a replacement for the British Lions versus an Overseas XV at Cardiff 1986. Also in 1986, he played for the Five Nations XV versus Overseas XV at Twickenham. He also played for Cardiff, Wales B and Barbarians.

Swansea put up a very courageous performance but eventually lost 37-22 to New Zealand on 21 October 1989. In the process, Swansea scored tries through Paul Arnold, Ian Davies and Kevin Hopkins with 2 penalties and 2 conversions from Mark Wyatt. The performance was put into perspective by Wales' subsequent 34-9 defeat to New Zealand.

Swansea score a try versus New Zealand to the obvious delight of the players.

Ian Davies sets up an attack with Robert Jones about to offer support. Ian scored one of Swansea's tries in a defiant fight-back after trailing 33-10 at half-time. Other Swansea players in view are, from left to right: Stuart Davies, Mike Morgan, Steve Williams and Arthur Emyr. Ian Davies played 196 games for Swansea between 1986/87 and 1995/96, scoring 71 tries. He also played for Wales B.

Mark Wyatt on the attack versus New Zealand. Other Swansea players in the picture are, from left to right: Billy James, Ian Davies, Alan Reynolds, Paul Arnold and Robert Jones.

Left: Mark Wyatt played on 10 occasions for Wales as a full-back, scoring 1 try, 21 penalties and 7 conversions. He played 299 games for Swansea between 1976/77 and 1991/92, scoring a club record total of 2,740 points (55 tries, 466 penalties, 6 drop goals and 552 conversions). He was the club's joint-top scorer with Arwel Thomas for points in a season (381 in 1984/85), until broken in 2003/04. He also played for Wales B and Barbarians. His father played for Pontypool and his sister has played rugby for the Welsh Women's team.

Right: Arthur Emyr played on 9 occasions for Wales as a wing, scoring 3 tries. He played 209 games for Swansea between 1980/81 and 1990/91 and in the process scored a club record 154 tries. He was chosen as Welsh rugby's Player of the Year in 1990. He also played for Llanelli, Cardiff, Wales B and Barbarians. Aside from rugby he represented Wales in athletics and came third in the 100 metres in the 1988 Welsh games. After his playing career, Arthur became involved in the media industry and was recently Head of Sport for BBC Wales.

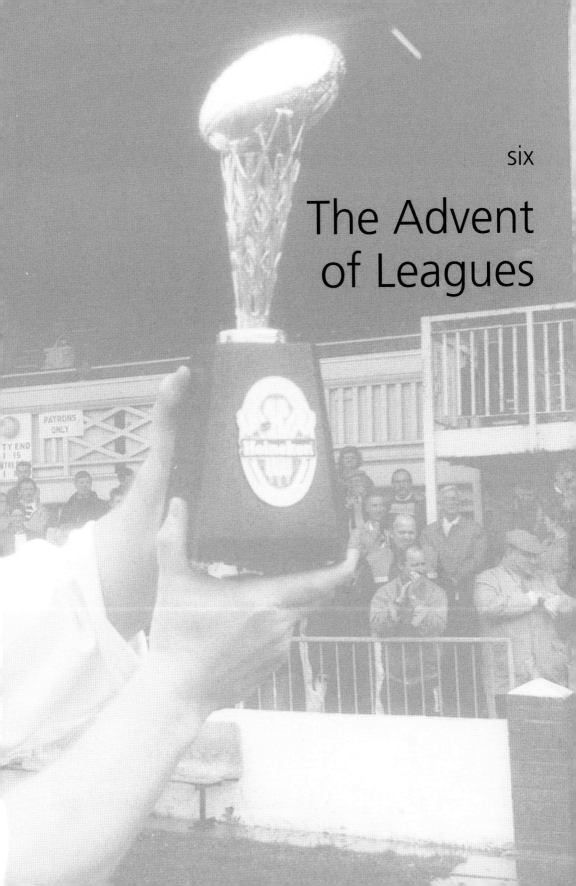

six

The Advent
of Leagues

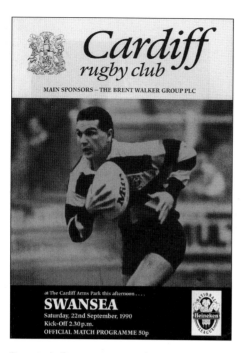

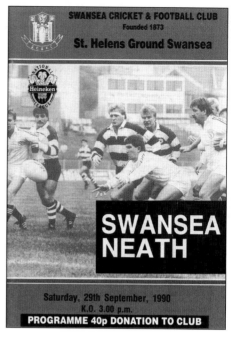

Swansea's first two games of Heineken League rugby were played on 22 September (Cardiff, away) and 29 September (Neath, home). Swansea lost both games, 28–13 to Cardiff and 23–14 to Neath. Swansea fared little better during the course of the season, finishing in eighth place in a top division comprised of ten teams. During the course of the season, Llanelli recorded their tenth consecutive win against Swansea, a record which was to extend to eleven wins the following season before Swansea were eventually victorious.

Mike Ruddock became director of coaching for the 1991/92 season. His playing career with Swansea (46 tries in 121 appearances between 1980/81 and 1985/86) had ended prematurely in September 1985 due to an accident at work. He quickly transformed a team which had finished eighth in 1990/91 to become champions in 1991/92 by injecting steel and self-belief into the more traditional Swansea flair. During his six seasons in charge, Swansea won the Welsh League twice, the Welsh Cup in 1995 and emerged victorious over world champions Australia in 1992. Mike took over as Wales coach from Steve Hansen in 2004. During his playing career, Mike had played for Wales B.

This is the championship-winning squad for 1991/92. From left to right, back row: Garin Jenkins, David Weatherley, David Joseph, Robin McBryde, Richard Moriarty, Paul Arnold, Richard Webster, Alan Reynolds, Keith Colclough, Ian Davies. Front row: Simon Davies, Bleddyn Taylor, Mark Titley, Anthony Clement, Robert Jones, Stuart Davies, Kevin Hopkins (captain), Scott Gibbs, Aled Williams, Ian Buckett, Stefan Jones.

HRH The Princess of Wales visited the Swansea primary schools' rugby display at St Helen's on 20 February 1992. Princess Diana was introduced to boys and girls from primary schools all over Swansea who were displaying their rugby skills, organized by the Welsh Rugby Union. This Royal visit was a tremendously memorable occasion and one of the highlights of the Swansea schools' distinguished history.

These are the six Swansea players who played for Wales versus France at Cardiff on 1 February 1992, a joint record representation last equalled by the club in 1908. From left to right: Stuart Davies, Scott Gibbs, Anthony Clement, Garin Jenkins, Robert Jones and Richard Webster.

The club's playing record for the 1991/92 season read as follows: played 44, won 31, drawn 1, lost 12, points for 928, points against 582. The team also won the *Western Mail* trophy as the highest try-scoring team in any division of the Heineken League.

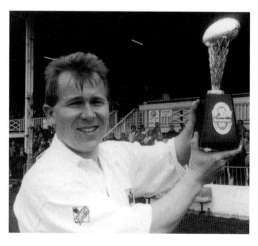

Captain Kevin Hopkins holds the Heineken League champions trophy for the 1991/92 season. Swansea won the title at Newport with a game to spare and ended their League campaign with a 23-23 draw at St Helen's on 9 May 1992 against Pontypool.

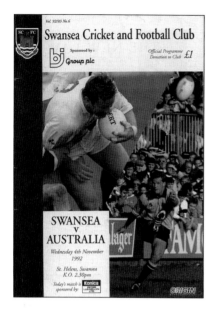

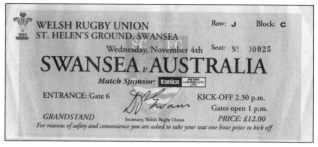

Whites on top of the world

Welsh champions tame Wallabies

Swansea recorded a victory of monumental proportions against reigning world champions Australia by 21 points to 6 on 4 November 1992, in front of a crowd of 10,150. This result represents the club's finest achievement since the Second World War and ranks alongside the 11–3 victory over New Zealand in 1935. Beforehand, Australia had targeted the Swansea front row as a potential weakness, containing as it did an unknown youngster and an elderly prop without any representative honours. At the first scrum, Keith Colclough's opposite number, Matt Ryan, 'popped out like a champagne cork'. This was a defining moment in the game, inspiring the entire Swansea team and leading to the downfall of the mighty champions. After the game, the Australian coach Bob Dwyer observed 'that was as good a performance as I can remember by a Welsh side'. As a result of the club's performance, a record-equalling six Swansea players represented Wales against Australia on 21 November. The players were: Stuart Davies, Scott Gibbs, Garin Jenkins, Robert Jones, Alan Reynolds (substitute) and Richard Webster.

Captain Stuart Davies leads out the Swansea team for their encounter with Australia. Stuart made a total of 244 appearances for Swansea between 1983/84 and 1997/98, scoring 84 tries. He captained the club in 1992/93 and the championship-winning 1993/94 season. He also represented Wales on 17 occasions as a back row forward. He played for Wales B and Barbarians. He is presently a BBC rugby commentator and summariser.

The victorious Swansea team line up before the game for the singing of the National Anthem. From left to right: Stuart Davies, Keith Colclough, Garin Jenkins, Chris Clark, Paul Arnold, Robert Jones, Aled Williams, Kevin Hopkins, Mark Titley, Richard Moriarty, Alan Reynolds, Simon Davies, Scott Gibbs, Anthony Clement and Richard Webster.

Scott Gibbs crosses for Swansea's opening try in the first half, surrounded by Australian players who appear dumbstruck at the ease with which the try was scored.

Garin Jenkins crosses for Swansea's second try in the second half, following an Australian tap-back at a line-out close to their own goal line.

Swansea's domination is reflected in the final scoreline, with their points coming from tries by Scott Gibbs and Garin Jenkins and two penalties, a drop goal and a conversion by Aled Williams. The Swansea team on that memorable day (in formation) was: Anthony Clement, Mark Titley, Kevin Hopkins, Scott Gibbs, Simon Davies, Aled Williams, Robert Jones, Chris Clark, Garin Jenkins, Keith Colclough, Paul Arnold, Richard Moriarty, Alan Reynolds, Stuart Davies (captain), Richard Webster.

Swansea's front-row domination was a critical factor in the success. From left to right: Keith Colclough, Garin Jenkins and Chris Clark who played the game of their lives. Whilst Colclough and Jenkins were experienced performers, they were joined by University College, Swansea student Clark in only his fifth game for the club.

Robert Jones releases his backs to set up an attack against Australia. Looking on are fellow Swansea players, from left to right: Stuart Davies, Richard Webster, Garin Jenkins and Alan Reynolds.

Brothers Robert (left) and Rhodri Jones seen here in opposition during the Neath versus Swansea Heineken League game on 30 January 1993. Rhodri was later to join Swansea and played 154 games between 1995/96 and 2002/03, scoring 28 tries.

Robert Jones (left) leading out the Swansea team versus Neath at St Helen's on 3 October 1992. He is seen here carrying out his daughter and team mascot Emily Nia. On the right, Emily Nia, is carried off the pitch prior to the start of the game by Neath's Uncle Rhodri.

Above: David Price first represented Swansea in the 1948/49 season whilst a student at University College of Wales, Aberystwyth. He appeared 22 times for the first XV and on numerous occasions for the Athletic XV, mainly during vacations. He once scored a 'hat trick' of tries against a visiting Aberavon XV. Succeeding Cliff Prosser as Swansea's seventh secretary in 1955, he served until 1992. He was later elected club president and is currently a life patron. He is a former headmaster and local magistrate.

Left: Kevin Hopkins played on 7 occasions for Wales as a centre. He played 178 games for Swansea between 1982/83 and 1992/93, scoring 40 tries, and captained the club in the championship-winning 1991/92 season. He also played for Neath, Cardiff, Wales B and Barbarians. He is the great-nephew of former All White and Wales international Thomas Hopkins. His brother, Cellan, also played for Swansea.

At the end of the 1992/93 season, a record four British Lions were selected from the club to tour New Zealand. From left: Robert Jones, Anthony Clement, Richard Webster and Scott Gibbs. Richard played on 13 occasions for Wales as a flanker, scoring 1 try. He played 97 games for Swansea between 1985/86 and 1993/94, scoring 38 tries, before moving to rugby league. He later returned to play rugby union with Bath and now coaches Bridgend. He also played for the Barbarians. Richard had made his debut for Wales as a teenager at the inaugural World Cup in 1987.

Swansea players in line-out action against Pontypridd in their league encounter at St Helen's on 9 April 1994, in a game won 17-6 by Swansea. The Swansea players, from left to right, are: Ian Buckett, Paul Arnold, Richard Moriarty, Alan Reynolds, Stuart Davies and Rob Appleyard.

This is the Heineken League champions squad of 1993/94. From left to right, back row: Rob Appleyard, Alan Reynolds, Richard Shaw, Mark Evans, Richard Moriarty, Paul Arnold, Steve Moore, Ian Buckett, Mike Morgan, Robin McBryde. Middle row: Baden Evans (team manager), Barry Clegg (coach), Paul Dowdeswell (physiotherapist), Trevor Cheeseman (fitness coach), Iestyn Lewis, Robbie Jones, David Weatherley, Sean Marshall, Anthony Wake, Steve Barclay, Jason Ball, Ian Davies, Byron Mugford (secretary), Roger Blyth (committee), Bernard Cajot (trainer), Colin Muxworthy (kit). Front row: Garin Jenkins, Robert Jones, Scott Gibbs, Mike Ruddock (director of coaching), Stuart Davies (captain), Anthony Clement, Aled Williams, Simon Davies.

The Swansea players celebrate their success from the St Helen's grandstand balcony.

The club's playing record for the 1993/94 season read as follows: played 41, won 27, lost 14, points for 948, points against 747.

Left: Mark Titley played on 15 occasions for Wales as a wing, scoring 4 tries. He played 260 games for Swansea between 1985/86 and 1993/94, scoring 120 tries. He also played for London Welsh, Bridgend, Wales B and Barbarians. His senior career started as an outside half before moving to the wing. He was also Welsh Rugby Player of the Year in 1984 whilst a Bridgend player.

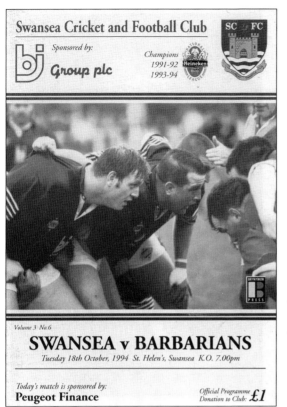

Swansea Cricket and Football Club

SC FC

Sponsored by:
bj Group plc

Champions
1991-92
1993-94

Heineken

Volume 3 No.6

SWANSEA v BARBARIANS

Tuesday 18th October, 1994 St. Helen's, Swansea K.O. 7.00pm

Today's match is sponsored by:
Peugeot Finance

Official Programme
Donation to Club: **£1**

Left: This was to be the occasion of the final Swansea versus Barbarians game. The match had been moved from the traditional Easter period due to end-of-season fixture congestion and weakened sides being selected by both teams. The fixture had commenced in 1901 and Swansea won the first 14 of the fixtures before a 0-0 draw in 1922 and a first victory for the Barbarians by 23-0 in 1923. The overall results summary was even with Swansea winning 40, Barbarians 41 and 2 drawn games. These Barbarians teams included many great international players from all over the world.

Below: This is the Swansea Under-21 squad that played against a New Zealand Under-21 team on 3 December 1994. From left to right, back row: Bob Thomas (trainer), Richard Terry, James Jackson, Steve Lawrence, Colin Gibson, Chris Morgan, Dawie Jacobs, Paul George, Jamie Lewis, Chris Atkinson, Chris Anthony, David Roberts (kit). Seated: Euros Evans, Lee Davies, Matthew Shepherd, Dean Thomas, Kevin Davies (captain), Neil James, Mark David, Greg Ellison. Front row: Warren Leach, Lyndon Griffiths, Chris Jones, Daniel Hawkins.

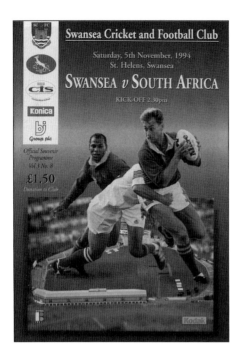
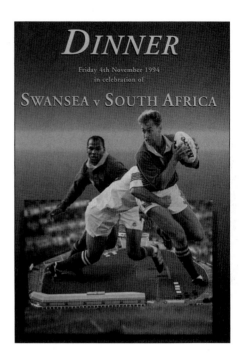

There was optimism regarding the visit of South Africa on 5 November 1994. The final score, however, comfortably represented a record defeat against a touring team – the All Whites losing by 78 points to 7. At half-time South Africa were only leading 13-7 but the tourists ran riot in the second half and scored 12 tries in all with full-back Joubert scoring 4 of them and converting 9. The stunned Swansea spectators were left to appreciate the skill, pace and tenacity of the tourists' backs and the dominance of their forwards.

Swansea's solitary points against South Africa came from this Simon Davies try that was converted by Aled Williams. Simon was a prolific try scorer on the wing for Swansea, scoring 124 tries in 207 appearances between 1990/91 and 1998/99. He also played for Wales B.

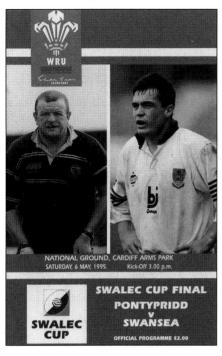

Swansea won the Welsh cup for the second occasion (following their success in 1978), defeating Pontypridd by 17 points to 12 in the final at the National Stadium on 6 May 1995. Swansea's points came from tries by Rob Appleyard and Stuart Davies and a penalty and 2 conversions by Aled Williams. Paul Arnold won the man of the match award.

This is Swansea's cup–winning squad of 1995. From left to right, back row: Mike Ruddock (director of coaching), Richard Llewellyn, Andy Moore, Paul Arnold, Richard Moriarty, Robbie Jones, Trevor Cheeseman (fitness coach). Middle row: Paul Dowdeswell (physiotherapist), Roger Blyth (chairman), Lyndon Griffiths, Alan Reynolds, Rob Appleyard, Shane McIntosh, Alan Harris, Christian Loader, Marcus Thomas, Colin Muxworthy (baggage master), Byron Mugford (secretary). Seated: Robert Jones, Roddy Boobyer, Keith Colclough, David Weatherley, Anthony Clement (captain), Garin Jenkins, Stuart Davies, Simon Davies, Aled Williams. Front row: Bernard Cajot (trainer), John Edwards (team attendant) and team mascot.

Line-out ball being secured by man of the match, Paul Arnold. Paul took 15 line-outs during the course of the cup final – as if to make a point to the Welsh selectors who had chosen his opposite number Greg Prosser for World Cup duty the following month in preference to him. Paul played for Wales on 16 occasions as a second row or number 8 forward and also made a total of 287 club appearances between 1987/88 and 1999/2000, scoring 38 tries. He also played for Wales B and Barbarians.

Anthony Clement crosses the line but the try is disallowed. Simon Davies is clearly convinced the try has been scored.

Above: Rob Appleyard about to score a try for Swansea in their cup final success. Rob played for Wales on 9 occasions as a flanker and also made a total of 139 club appearances between 1992/93 and 1999/2000, scoring 19 tries. He also played for Wales B, Barbarians, Sale, Cardiff and the Blues regional team.

Left: Captain Anthony Clement prepares to hold the cup aloft following the team's triumph in the final.

The Swansea players celebrate their cup success. Players, from left to right: Christian Loader, Andy Moore, Simon Davies, Paul Arnold, David Weatherley, Aled Williams, Rob Appleyard and Stuart Davies.

Captain Anthony Clement holds the cup aloft as the entire squad celebrates.

MUNSTER
V.
SWANSEA

Thomond Park, Limerick
Wednesday, November 1st, 1995
kick-off 2.30 p.m.

Swansea's first venture into the European Cup resulted in a narrow 17 points to 13 defeat away to Munster on 1 November 1995. Swansea's points came from an Alan Harris try and 2 penalties and a conversion from Aled Williams. Swansea went on to defeat Castres by 22 points to 10 at St Helen's with tries from Alan Harris and Garin Jenkins and 4 Aled Williams penalties. This was a very ill-tempered match with the Castres president threatening to take his team off the field. As a consequence of Castres beating Munster by 19 points to 12, Swansea qualified for the semi-finals.

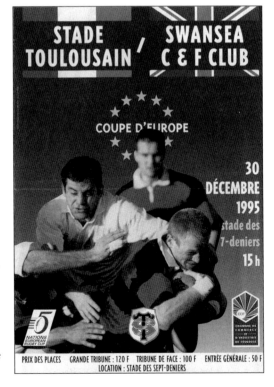

Swansea's one and only European Cup semi-final was played at Toulouse on 30 December 1995 and resulted in a heavy 30 points to 3 defeat. An Aled Williams penalty represented Swansea's only scoring. Toulouse had only been defeated at home on one occasion in eight years and dominated the game in front of a 10,000 partisan crowd. Andy Moore, Swansea's second row forward, suffered a serious injury in the game that was to sideline him until 15 November 1997.

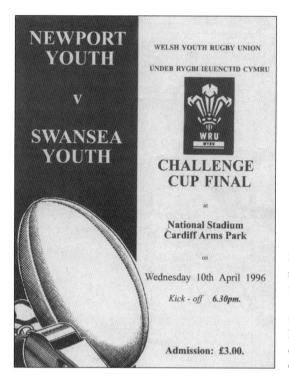

NEWPORT
YOUTH

v

SWANSEA
YOUTH

WELSH YOUTH RUGBY UNION

UNDEB RYGBI IEUENCTID CYMRU

WRU

CHALLENGE
CUP FINAL

at

National Stadium
Cardiff Arms Park

on

Wednesday 10th April 1996

Kick - off 6.30pm.

Admission: £3.00.

Swansea, who had enjoyed an unbeaten season, edged home by 10 points to 9 in the Welsh Youth Cup final on 10 April 1996. This was Swansea's first success in the twenty-four-year history of the knockout competition. Swansea's scores came from tries by prop Andrew May and centre Huw Thomas.

Swansea captain Chris Wells (right) holds the Welsh Youth Cup aloft at the National Stadium, Cardiff. Chris had only just returned from captaining Wales in the FIRA Under-19 World Cup, losing in the final to Argentina. Chris went on to play more than 100 games for the club, despite many injuries, and featured in the Neath/Swansea Ospreys regional team in 2003/04. He joined Aberavon for the 2004/05 season.

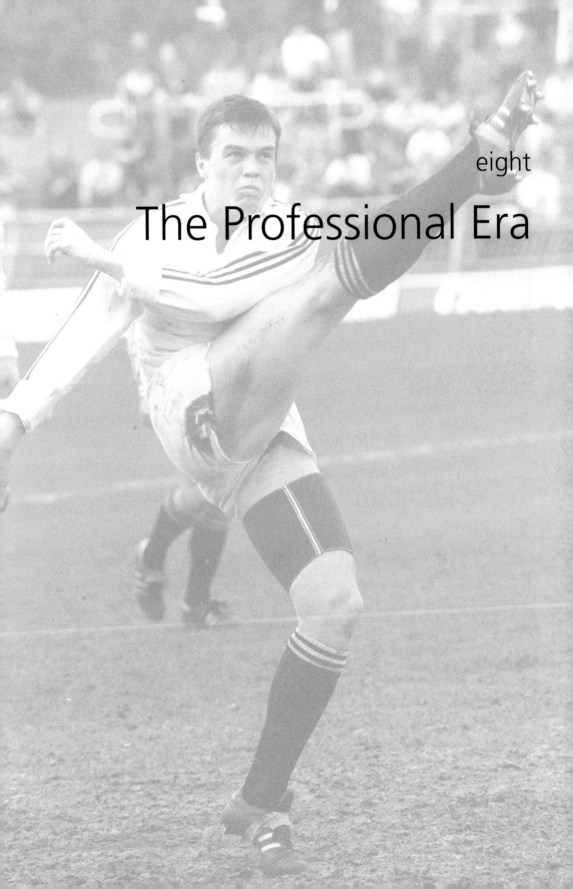

eight

The Professional Era

Mike James played a total of 163 games for Swansea between 1968/69 and 1974/75, scoring 13 tries. He was a tough, uncompromising second row forward. After retirement he joined the club committee before becoming chairman in 1991. With the advent of professionalism in the mid-1990s he became one of the club's major benefactors, together with Robert Davies and Roger Blyth.

Richard Moriarty holds the club's all-time record for appearances (472) in a career spanning over twenty years from 1976/77 to 1997/98, in which he also scored 32 tries. He was club captain for three consecutive seasons: 1986/87, 1987/88 and 1988/89. He played on 22 occasions for Wales, either as a second row or back row forward scoring 2 tries and captained Wales on 7 occasions, including at the inaugural World Cup in 1987. He also played for Wales B. He was recently team manager of Swansea. He is the elder brother of fellow All White and Wales international, Paul.

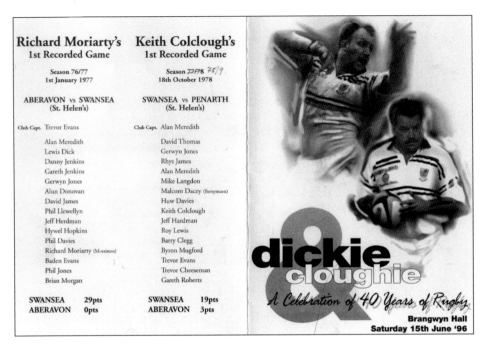

Richard Moriarty's 1st Recorded Game	Keith Colclough's 1st Recorded Game
Season 76/77 1st January 1977	Season 77/78 78/9 18th October 1978
ABERAVON vs SWANSEA (St. Helen's)	SWANSEA vs PENARTH (St. Helen's)
Club Capt. Trevor Evans	Club Capt. Alan Meredith
Alan Meredith	David Thomas
Lewis Dick	Gerwyn Jones
Danny Jenkins	Rhys James
Gareth Jenkins	Alan Meredith
Gerwyn Jones	Mike Langdon
Alun Donovan	Malcom Dacey (Bonymaen)
David James	Huw Davies
Phil Llewellyn	Keith Colclough
Jeff Herdman	Jeff Hardman
Hywel Hopkins	Roy Lewis
Phil Davies	Barry Clegg
Richard Moriarty (Morriston)	Byron Mugford
Baden Evans	Trevor Evans
Phil Jones	Trevor Cheeseman
Brian Morgan	Gareth Roberts
SWANSEA 29pts ABERAVON 0pts	SWANSEA 19pts ABERAVON 3pts

dickie & cloughie

A Celebration of 40 Years of Rugby

**Brangwyn Hall
Saturday 15th June '96**

This game was arranged in recognition of Swansea's two record appearance holders Richard Moriarty and Keith Colclough. Keith played for Swansea on 431 occasions in a career spanning twenty years from 1978/79 to 1997/98 in which he scored 13 tries. He was very unfortunate never to have received international recognition, having been a highly respected prop forward for many years. He played for the Barbarians.

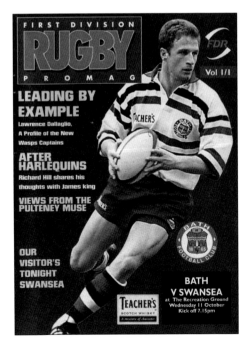

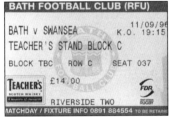

On Wednesday 11 September 1996, Swansea travelled to Bath for a mid-week Anglo Welsh game. Bath's victory by 87 points to 15 represented a record defeat for Swansea that still stands today. The Swansea team included current and future internationals Scott Gibbs, Mark Taylor, Anthony Clement, Aled Williams, Colin Charvis, Ian Buckett, Rob Appleyard, Steve Moore and veteran Richard Moriarty, but were overwhelmed by a Bath team including former rugby league players Henry Paul and Jason Robinson.

Aled Williams is Swansea's fourth most prolific points scorer. He scored a total of 1,505 points (73 tries, 215 penalties, 16 drop goals and 240 conversions) in 217 appearances between 1983/84 and 1997/98. He played on 2 occasions for Wales. He also played for Bridgend and Barbarians.

John Plumtree joined Swansea as coach for the commencement of the 1997/98 season. During his five seasons at the club, Swansea won the Welsh League in 1997/98, the Welsh-Scottish League in 2000/01 and the Welsh Cup in 1999. As a player, Plum played in the back row and made his debut in 1985 for Taranaki, playing for them on 40 occasions before playing 15 games for Hawke's Bay. He was an All Black trialist in 1989. Later he played for seven years in South Africa, playing 80 times for Natal and representing South Africa at sevens rugby.

The 1997/98 squad. From left to right, back row: Richard Rees, Andrew Grabham, Stuart Davies, Danzi Niblo, Paul Arnold, James Griffiths, Andy Moore, Colin Charvis, Matthew Back, Mark Taylor. Middle row: Bernard Cajot, Tudor Jeremiah, Ian Chesterfield, John Edwards, Stuart Johnson, Huw Thomas, Chris Wells, Chris Anthony, Richard Field, Paul Moriarty, Tyrone Maullin, Ian Buckett, Anthony Clement, Dean Thomas, Baden Evans, Kevin Hopkins, Trevor Cheeseman, Paul Dowdeswell. Front row: Robbie Jones, Scott Gibbs, Rhodri Jones, David Weatherley, Christian Loader, John Plumtree, Garin Jenkins, Arwel Thomas, Andy Booth, Simon Davies, Rob Appleyard, Alan Harris.

Swansea took on the Northern Bulls Super 12 team from South Africa on 14 January 1998 in the new WRU Challenge Trophy and the end result was a thrilling 34-34 draw. Swansea's points came from Paul Arnold, Richard Rees and Arwel Thomas tries, 2 penalty tries, a penalty and 3 conversions to Arwel Thomas. Swansea defeated both their other foreign opponents in the Trophy competition, Rosario 51-31 (10 January) and Rugby Canada 38-29 (18 January).

Anthony Clement played on 37 occasions for Wales as a utility back, scoring 3 tries and 1 drop goal. He played 246 games for Swansea between 1985/86 and 1998/99, scoring 61 tries, captaining the club in 1994/95 and 1995/96. He also toured with the 1989 British Lions to Australia (as replacement) and to New Zealand in 1993. He also played for Wales B and Barbarians. He won the man of the match award in the 1987 Welsh Cup final.

On 2 May 1998 Swansea eclipsed Bridgend by 71 points to 19 in a Heineken League game at St Helen's. The biggest cheer of the day, though, was reserved for a few minutes before the end of play when substitute hooker Dean Colclough made his club debut – and joined dad Keith on the field of play for what was to be his 431st and final appearance for Swansea! This is probably a unique record for Swansea and will long be remembered by proud father and son (illustrated with dad on the left) and supporters alike.

Paul Moriarty scores one of his two tries to send Swansea onto a decisive 45 points to 27 win at Pontypridd to be crowned 1997/98 League Champions. Paul was a prolific try-scorer for Swansea, gaining 113 touchdowns in 299 games. He scored 25 tries in the 1985/86 season – an all-time club record for a forward.

In the end Swansea comfortably won the league by 6 points. Their record in the competition was: played 14, won 11, drawn 2, lost 1, points for 569, points against 263 with 11 bonus points for a grand total of 46. Swansea players celebrate on the Sardis Road stand balcony. From left to right: Rob Appleyard, Andy Booth, Paul Arnold, Andy Moore, Arwel Thomas and Simon Davies. The club's playing record for the entire 1997/98 season read as follows: played 34, won 23, drawn 3, lost 8, points for 1,232, points against 738.

John Plumtree followed the achievement of his predecessor Mike Ruddock in coaching Swansea to a league championship victory in his first season in charge. Here he is seen celebrating with Scott Gibbs (left) and Garin Jenkins.

Swansea, along with Cardiff, embarked upon a 'rebel' season in 1998/99 involving a series of friendly games against English premiership teams on a home-and-away basis. The club had refused to sign a ten-year loyalty agreement with the WRU and consequently were not allowed to play in the Welsh Premier Division. Here Swansea's Roger Blyth (left) and Cardiff's Gareth Davies explain the clubs' decisions at a press conference.

This is Swansea's 'rebel' squad of 1998/99. Scott Gibbs took over from Garin Jenkins as captain and remained in charge for five consecutive seasons until relinquishing the post during 2002/03 only to take over as captain again later that season.

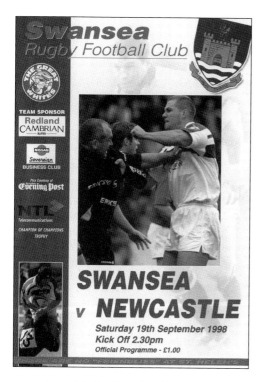

Above left: On Saturday 19 September Swansea entertained Newcastle in a game billed as the clash of the 'champion of champions', given both teams had won their respective national leagues the previous season. Swansea won by 26 points to 14, with an Andy Booth try and 6 penalties and a drop goal from Arwel Thomas.

Above right: Scott Gibbs in typical action versus Newcastle, displaying his obvious strength.

MEMBER OF THE WELSH RUGBY UNION
WEST WALES RUGBY UNION
CARMARTHEN COUNTY AND LLANELLI
AND DISTRICT RUGBY UNION
AMMAN VALLEY AND DISTRICT YOUTH RUGBY UNION
AND THE WELSH YOUTH RUGBY UNION

CLWB RYGBI'R AMAN

AMMAN UNITED

RUGBY CLUB

Cwmamman Park, Garnant

~ Official Match Programme ~

In a cup game that had been delayed by twenty-four hours due to rain, Swansea defeated Amman United by 100 points to 7, a record winning margin for the club. Swansea scored a total of 16 tries, of which 10 were successfully converted. This remains the only occasion for the Whites to score a century of points in a single game. It is worth noting that in 1895/96 Swansea only scored 172 points in an entire season comprising 30 games!

Colin Charvis in action during the cup game against Amman United. Colin has played on 71 occasions, to date, for Wales as a back row forward, scoring 13 tries, captaining them on 21 occasions. He played 168 games for Swansea between 1994/95 and 2002/03, scoring 62 tries and toured with the 2001 British Lions to Australia. He joined Swansea from London Welsh and played for French Second Division club side Tarbes in 2003/04 after the 2003 World Cup before joining Newcastle for the 2004/05 season. Colin has also played for the Barbarians.

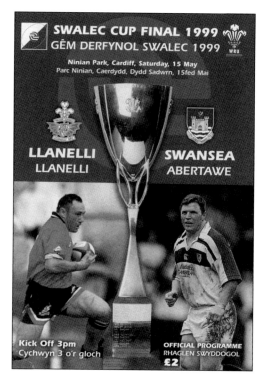

Swansea won the Welsh Cup for the third occasion by overwhelming Llanelli by 37 points to 10, a record winning margin for a final. In a clash labelled as the 'rebels' versus 'loyalists', an awesome scrum and a superior line-out gave Swansea the platform to win. Swansea's points came from tries by Colin Charvis (2), Tyrone Maullin and Dean Thomas with Arwel Thomas adding 3 conversions, a penalty and 2 drop goals with Lee Davies also adding a conversion.

The Swansea team line-up for the cup final. From left to right: Scott Gibbs, Mark Taylor, David Weatherley, Rhodri Jones, Arwel Thomas, Ben Evans, Garin Jenkins, Darren Morris, Andy Moore, Tyrone Maullin, Richard Rees, Paul Moriarty, Lee Jones, Matthew Robinson and Colin Charvis.

Dean Thomas celebrates his try in the cup final. Dean had been expected to start the game due to an injury to Colin Charvis. The team announcement shortly before kick off surprised everyone when Charvis was named to start. Deano came on as a second-half replacement for Charvis.

With construction of the Millenium Stadium taking place, the final was played at Cardiff City's Ninian Park ground in front of a 14,500 sell-out crowd. Rarely has success over the old enemy tasted sweeter for Swansea. In a fitting finale Scott Gibbs, who left the field to a standing ovation when he was replaced late on, stepped up to lift the Welsh Cup in front of Swansea's jubilant fans. Arwel Thomas was named as man of the match. Here, the jubilant players display the cup and medals in front of the grandstand.

This is the Swansea squad celebrating their cup success.

1998/99 fixtures

1998				1999			
Sep 5	W Hartlepool	(h)	32-26	Jan 2	Richmond	(h)	57-3
13	Wasps	(a)	28-18	9	Cardiff	(a)	19-40
19	Newcastle	(h)	26-14	16	Wasps	(h)	27-13
26	Richmond	(a)	13-28	24	Saracens	(a)	29-59
Oct 3	Saracens	(h)	25-32	30	Newport (Cup)	(h)	60-38
10	Gloucester	(h)	27-16	Feb 7	W Hartlepool	(a)	28-27
17	London Irish	(a)	38-20	13	Northampton	(h)	58-24
20	Northampton	(a)	34-18	27	Bridgend (Cup)	(a)	43-16
24	Amman Utd (Cup)	(a)	100-7	Mar 13	Newcastle	(a)	25-43
31	Sale	(a)	22-24	27	Ebbw Vale (Cup)	(h)	42-14
Nov 7	London Scottish	(h)	76-5	Apr 3	London Scottish	(h)	12-27
13	Bath	(a)	7-34	18	Cross Keys (Cup)		60-3
20	Leicester	(a)	20-7	20	Bedford	(h)	46-31
28	Crynant (Cup)	(a)	48-0	24	London Irish	(h)	34-31
Dec 5	Cardiff	(h)	31-15	May 1	Harlequins	(a)	Cancelled
12	Harlequins	(h)	32-18	4	Gloucester	(a)	10-37
19	Risca (Cup)	(a)	57-8	8	Leicester	(h)	34-22
20	Bedford	(a)	28-14	15	Llanelli (Cup final)	(N)	**37-10**
26	Bath	(h)	50-17				

This represents the outcome of the club's 1998/99 'rebel' season. Both Swansea and Cardiff returned to the Welsh domestic league for the following 1999/2000 season.

'I see WE we won again!'

Left and above left: A local derby between Swansea and Llanelli evokes all sorts of passion for both sets of supporters. Intense rivalry has existed since their very first encounter at Felinfoel on 5 February 1876 when the result was a draw. In the 364 games played between the teams, results remain pretty even with Llanelli recording 167 wins, Swansea 155 with 41 drawn and an abandoned game.

Swansea had become known as The Great Whites and their mascot Fergal the Shark (right) could be seen at home matches on a regular basis. Fergal rivaled the City's other famous mascot, namely Swansea City's Cyril the Swan.

Robert Jones played on 54 occasions for Wales as a scrum half, scoring 4 tries, captaining them on 5 occasions. Often his Wales appearances were behind a struggling pack of forwards; there is no telling how he may have blossomed with a constant supply of good ball. He made his Swansea debut as a schoolboy and went on to play 286 games between 1983/84 and 2001/02, scoring 50 tries, captaining them in 1989/90 and 1990/91. He was also the club's top scorer in the inaugural Heineken League season of 1990/91. He played for the 1989 and 1993 British Lions as well as playing for the British Lions versus an Overseas XV at Cardiff in 1986 and for the Home Unions versus France in 1989. He also played for Bristol, Cardiff, Wales B and Barbarians. He is the son-in-law of Clive Rowlands.

Paul Moriarty played on 21 occasions for Wales as a back row forward, scoring 4 tries. He played 299 games for Swansea between 1983/84 and 2001/02, scoring 113 tries. He also played rugby league for Widnes and Halifax and represented Wales on 15 occasions and Great Britain twice. He played for Wales with elder brother Richard on 9 occasions, all overseas, and has also played for Wales B and Barbarians. He recently coached Swansea and has been part of the Scarlets regional coaching team for 2003/04 and 2004/05.

This is the playing squad in the 2000/01 league championship season. From left to right, back row: Richard Rees, Ben Evans, Geraint Lewis, Hywel Jenkins, Lee Jones, James Griffiths, Tyrone Maullin, Paul Moriarty, Andrew Grabham, Steve Winn, Matthew Robinson. Middle row: -?-, Phil Richards (fitness), Cerith Rees, Sililo Martens, Dean Thomas, Kevin Morgan, Gavin Henson, James Bater, Mark Taylor, Shaun Payne, Chris Anthony, Arwel Thomas, -?-, -?-, -?-. Front row: Rhodri Jones, David Weatherley, Gareth Noble, Gareth Mason, Clive Griffiths (defence coach), Scott Gibbs (captain), John Plumtree (director of coaching), Colin Charvis, Baden Evans (team manager), Chris Wells, Garin Jenkins, Darren Morris.

The Swansea squad celebrate their Welsh-Scottish league success at the end of the 2000/01 season. The club's playing record for the season read as follows: played 33, won 25, lost 8, points for 1,238, points against 610.

This photograph demonstrates the success of the club's rugby academy that has been established for talented up-and-coming rugby players in the area. No fewer than twenty-one players (pictured above) were selected in the 2000/01 season to represent Wales at either under-17, 19 or 21 age group levels. The likes of Johnathan Thomas, Paul Mackey, Gareth Swales and Matthew Brayley (who are all featured in the photograph) are now part of the senior squad. Gavin Henson (who does not feature above) went on to be capped for Wales at the end of the season in Japan.

Swansea Schools under-15 centenary squad 2000/01. This side became Dewar Shield winners.
From left to right, back row: Craig Thomas, Peter Richards, Daniel Lloyd-Jones, Gareth Lynch, Alun Jones, Stephen Rogers, Rory Gallagher, Jonathan Rees, Ben Lewis, Sean Hopkins.
Middle row: Keith Day, Vernon Richards, Roger Davies, Ian Milne, Roland Emmanuel, Jane Clayton, Greg Cunniffe, Carl Ackland, Matthew Roblin, Sam John, Ian Ware, Paul Milne, Edward Carr, Luke Jones, Marc Jones, Derrick Howells, Trevor Cheeseman, Pat Dwan, Peter Richards, Leighton Crook. Seated: Keiron Jones, Ian Brooks, Warren Fury (captain), David Watts, Tom Cheeseman, James Littlehales, Terry Stone. Ground: Stuart Allen, Leigh Bevan, Mark Evans, Anthony Gills.

Swansea Schools centenary tour squad, South Africa 2001. From left to right, back row: Craig Dalling, Rhodri Davies, Alun Jones, James Littlehales, Nick Bowen, Greg Jervis, Mike Attwell, Liam Davies. Third row: Joe Hixson, Anthony Carmichael, Gareth Lynch, Craig Thomas, David Lynch, Rory Gallagher, Gareth Crabbe. Second row: Richard Jones, Tom Cushion, Anthony Morris, Tom Liney, Mark Robins, Aled Davies, Paul Beynon, Jordan Jackson, Ben Bonham, David Watts. Front row: Andrew Williams, Chris Strick (captain), Pat Dwan, Roger Davies, Keith Day, Roland Emanuel, Derrick Howells, Ian Milne, Mitchell Ford, Warren Fury.

Swansea Schools' senior Wales internationals (left to right): Len Blyth, J. Idwal Rees, Anthony Clement, John Faull, Richard Webster, Harry Payne, Phil Llewellyn, Richard Moriarty, Stephen Jones, Horace Phillips, Malcolm Dacey, Mervyn Davies, Stuart Davies, Paul Arnold, Chris Anthony, Billy Hullin, John Leleu, Jack John, Andrew Lloyd, Geoff Wheel, Roger Blyth, Haydn Mainwaring, Spencer John.

Bernard Cajot (left) and John Edwards retired from club duties at the end of the 1999/2000 season. Bernard played as a scrum half on 27 occasions between 1950/51 and 1955/56 and later became trainer and kitman, providing over fifty years of loyal service to the club. John had been involved with the club over thirty years in the capacity of coach driver, supporters' club member and latterly kit man and team attendant.

Swansea equalled their 1993 record with four players selected for the British Lions tour of 2001. Clockwise from top left: Darren Morris, Colin Charvis, Scott Gibbs (replacement) and Mark Taylor. Darren Morris has played on 18 occasions for Wales as a prop, scoring 1 try. He played 116 games for Swansea between 1998/99 and 2002/03, scoring 6 tries. He played for Neath prior to Swansea and for Leicester in 2003/04 and 2004/05 and also played for the Barbarians.

A record nine Wales Under-16s caps were awarded to Swansea boys in the 2001/02 season. Eight Swansea boys played in the match versus Italy at St Helen's, beating the record of seven who played versus England in 1914. From left to right, standing: Ian Milne (schools secretary), Trevor Cheeseman (schools chairman), Stephen Rogers, Alun Wyn Jones, Rory Gallagher, Gareth Lynch, Keith Day (team manager). Seated: James Littlehales, Warren Fury, David Watts, Tom Cheeseman, Craig Thomas.

This is the All Whites former players association committee gathering at their annual dinner in October 2001. From left to right, inset: Dil Johnson. Standing: Meirion Phillips, Neil Jones, W. John Davies, John Blyth, Dr Howard Bowen, Brian Jones (honorary secretary). Seated: Terry Morgan, Billy Williams, Geoff Wheel (president), David Price (chairman), Wilfred Jones (honorary treasurer), Vic Trew.

nine

The End
of an Era

DARK DAYS AHEAD AS WHITES HIT CASH CRISIS

Above left: Garin Jenkins played on 58 occasions for Wales as a hooker, scoring 2 tries. He played 223 games for Swansea between 1991/92 and 2002/03, scoring 28 tries and captaining them in 1996/97 and 1997/98. Garin's formidable skills and 100 per cent commitment helped give the Swansea pack a steely resolve and a formidable reputation. He is Swansea's record Welsh cap holder, and played in three World Cups (1991, 1995 and 1999). He was the last coalminer to play for Wales. He coached the Neath/Swansea Ospreys regional academy team for 2003/04, and 2004/05.

Above right: Swansea announced on 10 March 2003 that it would be applying for a temporary administration order as a result of the onset of regional rugby in Wales. This was a reaction to the WRU's plans to reduce funding to the Premier Division clubs from almost £1 million to just £50,000 a year.

Arwel Thomas is Swansea's third most prolific points scorer. He scored a total of 1,965 points (39 tries, 338 penalties, 32 drop goals and 330 conversions) in 152 appearances between 1993/94 and 2001/02. He also played on 23 occasions for Wales, scoring 216 points (12 tries, 32 penalties and 30 conversions). He was the club's joint-top scorer with Mark Wyatt for points in a season (381 in 1997/98) until exceeded by Luke Richards in the 2003/04 season. He also played for Neath, Bristol, Pau and Barbarians, and has joined Llanelli Scarlets for 2004/05. He played on permit for Llandovery against Swansea at St Helen's on 16 October 2004.

Left: Mark Taylor has played, to date, on 47 occasions for Wales as a centre, scoring 10 tries and captaining them twice. He played 173 games for Swansea between 1995/96 and 2002/03, scoring 67 tries. He played for the 2001 British Lions in Australia. He also played for Pontypool prior to joining Swansea and for the Scarlets regional team in 2003/04 and 2004/05. He was Welsh Rugby Player of the Year in 2000.

Below: Aerial photograph of St Helen's ground as it is today. The cricket square (scene of many Glamorgan cricket achievements and Sir Garry Sobers' 6 sixes in one over in 1968) and the beach is clearly in view. Whether Swansea will continue to play at St Helen's is still to be determined. St Helen's remained as Swansea's home ground for a semi-professional team in 2003/04 and 2004/05 and has been a venue for some of the Neath/Swansea Ospreys games in the new regional structure of the game in Wales.

The Neath/Swansea Ospreys regional team was launched on 24 July 2003. Shane Williams (left) and regional captain Scott Gibbs parade the new team's jersey at the official launch. Scott decided to announce his retirement on his thirty-third birthday (23 January 2004) during the course of the season but returned for one more game to assist the team when many of the squad was unavailable. The team logo is shown on the right, depicting an osprey and a Maltese cross.

Scott Gibbs played on 53 occasions for Wales as a centre, scoring 10 tries and captaining them on a single occasion. He played 195 games for Swansea between 1991/92 and 2002/03, scoring 72 tries. Scott is the only triple British Lion produced by Swansea (1993, 1997 and 2001), his man-of-the-series performance in South Africa with the British Lions in 1997 culminating in his winning the Welsh Sports Personality of the Year award. He also captained the club for five consecutive seasons (1998/99 to 2002/03) – a record shared with two of the greatest names in the club's history, namely Billy Bancroft and Billy Trew. He was the youngest ever Welsh Rugby Player of the Year in 1991, while with Neath. He also played for the Barbarians.

ten

New
Beginnings

Above left: Luke Richards joined Swansea for 2003/04, having previously been a prolific scorer for Neath and Caerphilly. The diminutive outside half was the club's top scorer in 2003/04 with 394 points, comprising 7 tries, 61 penalties, 8 drop goals and 76 conversions. This represented a club record number of points in a season, beating Mark Wyatt (1984/85) and Arwel Thomas (1997/98) previous record of 381. Luke was also the record points scorer in the Premiership Division in 2003/04. In the 2004/05 season, Luke has already amassed 100 league points by the middle of October.

Above right: Gavin Vaughan Evans had played on 4 occasions for Swansea in 2002/03. He became a regular in 2003/04, following the advent of regional rugby. He played both as a number 8 and second row forward, securing a steady supply of line-out ball. He captained the team on a number of occasions in the absence of Richard Francis and Matthew Brayley.

After more than twenty years of deliberation, the Morfa development was confirmed in 2003. The new retail and leisure park facility will include the 20,000 capacity White Rock stadium , which is intended to become the home for both Swansea City FC and the Neath/Swansea Ospreys regional rugby team from the commencement of the 2005/06 season. The future of St Helen's as a home for Swansea RFC remains in doubt but it is unlikely that the club will play its Premiership rugby at this new stadium. The picture shows the current state of construction as at October 2004.

eleven

David Price's Swansea XV (1945-2004)

The nomination of a post Second World War Swansea XV has been somewhat less difficult than the choice of a team for the previous era (1873-1945) in as much as I saw, knew, and even played a limited number of games with two of the nominees.

It was, nevertheless, still difficult and I have sought to create a balanced side in addition to one of ability. For example, the nomination of Mark Wyatt at full-back, for amongst his talents were exceptional goal-kicking feats over many seasons.

There are many other names that could be placed parallel with those in the nominated XV. This is but the opinion of one person and will I am sure stimulate both debate and controversy!

Full-back: Mark Wyatt. Three-quarters: Mark Titley, Mark Taylor, Scott Gibbs, Dewi Bebb. Half-backs: David Richards, Robert Jones.

Front row: Phil Llewellyn, Garin Jenkins, 'Billy' Williams. Second row: Richard Moriarty, Geoff Wheel. Back row: Paul Moriarty, Mervyn Davies, Clem Thomas.

Mervyn Davies is my nomination as captain of this team. Perhaps not surprisingly, all fifteen players were full Welsh internationals, and eight were British Lions.

Ultimately, choices were made on the basis of number of games played for the first XV. This criterion eliminated such distinguished players as Norman Gale, David Young, Stuart Evans and Maurice Colclough from selection.

D.P. Price, life patron.

The official Swansea RFC website can be found at www.swansearfc.co.uk. The site features include brief details of the club's long and distinguished history, news updates, profiles of the playing squad, results/fixtures and a lively supporters' chat forum.

The independent Swansea RFC supporters website can be found at www.thewhitesrugby.com. The site is managed by Stuart Rees, a dedicated All Whites supporter. The site features include regular news updates, match reports, fantasy rugby competitions and a supporters' forum where all are welcomed. There is also the very popular Mo's Tavern for the best jokes that are guaranteed to put a smile on your face.

Other local titles published by Tempus

Swansea RFC 1873-1945

BLEDDYN HOPKINS

The All Whites were founded in 1873 and became one of the eleven founder clubs of the Welsh Rugby Union in 1881. Swansea Rugby Club's history is renowned the world over for its many achievements. This volume traces the club's development from its formation through to the end of the Second World War. It gives a fascinating insight into the club and features team photographs, player portraits, action shots and many items of club memorabilia.

7524 2721 0

Swansea Town Football Club 1912-1964

RICHARD SHEPHERD

This collection of over 250 old photographs and assorted memorabilia illustrates the history of Swansea Town Football Club from its beginnings in 1912 until 1964, when The Swans came within forty-five minutes of reaching an FA Cup Final at Wembley. This book contains many action shots and behind-the-scenes pictures recording the formation of the club and the players that made the club great.

7524 1133 0

If you are interested in purchasing other books published by Tempus, or in case you have difficulty finding any Tempus books in your local bookshop, you can also place orders directly through our website

www.tempus-publishing.com